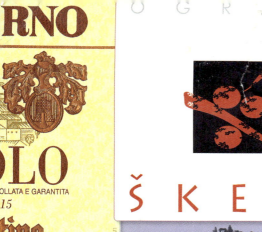

RNO

OLO
...llata e garantita
...15
...tino

ine da
...i conterno s.a.s.s.
...la
14.5% vol

Miani

ŠKERK

I FAVATI
PIETRAMARA
ETICHETTA BIANC.
FIANO DI AVELLINO
DENOMINAZIONE DI ORIGINE CONTROLLATA E GARANTITA
RISERVA

MW01487217

SALVIONI
2022
imbottigliato all'origine
da Azienda Agricola
«LA CERBAIOLA»
di SALVIONI GIULIO
MONTALCINO
ITALIA

GROSJEAN
VALLÉE D'AOSTE
DENOMINAZIONE DI ORIGINE CONTROLLATA
PETITE ARVINE
2023

BARBERA D'ALBA
DENOMINAZIONE DI ORIGINE CONTROLLATA
Campass
2021
IMBOTTIGLIATO ALL'ORIGINE DA
Az.Agr. F.lli Cigliuti
NEIVE - ITALIA

GAJA
Contenuto netto
litri 0,70   Gradi 13
1859
VINO
BARBARESCO
DENOMINAZIONE DI ORIGINE CONTROLLATA
IMBOTTIGLIATO DAL PRODUTTORE ALL'ORIGINE

CHARDONNAY

ARBORINA

Piero Busso

BARBARESCO
DENOMINAZIONE DI ORIGINE CONTROLLATA E GARANTITA
SAN STUNET

FLACCIANELLO®
DELLA PIEVE   2020
INTEGRALMENTE PRODOTTO E
IMBOTTIGLIATO ALL'ORIGINE NELLA
AZIENDA AGRICOLA FONTODI

MONTEVERTINE
LE PERGOLE TORTE
1990 Riserva
Vino prodotto con uva Sangiovese raccolta
nella vigna "Le Pergole Torte" selezionata
e vinificata da Sergio Manetti con la
collaborazione del cantiniere Bruno Bini
ed il maestro assaggiatore Giulio Gambelli.
L'invecchiamento e l'imbottigliamento sono
avvenuti presso la Fattoria di Montevertine.
Radda in Chianti
Vino da tavola di Toscana
3 litri   13%
NON DISPERDERE IL VETRO NELL'AMBIENTE

2022 I PIN
DI CORSANO

TERENZUOLA

GIACOMO FENOCCHIO

PRODOTTO IN ITALIA

Barolo
...ZIONE DI ORIGINE CONTROLLATA E GARANTITA

...llata e Garantita

Azienda Agricola

Bottled

...icoltore

...orra - Italia

15% BY VOL.

INDEHOLDER SULFITTER

BRUNELLO
DI
MONTALCINO
DENOMINAZIONE DI ORIGINE
CONTROLLATA
E
GARANTITA

n°:   /2 200

VIGNAVECCHIA
1876
CHIANTI CLASSICO   GRAN SELEZIONI
Denominazione di origine controllata e garantita
100% Sangiovese

BROVIA

BAROLO
Denominazione di Origine Controllata e Gara...
2020
RED WINE - PRODUCT OF ITALY
IMBOTTIGLIATO DA - BOTTLED BY
AZIENDA AGRICOLA BROVIA SSA - CASTIGLIONE FALLETTO
NET CONT. 750 ML ℮   PRODOTTO IN ITALIA - L 06/24   ALC 14.5% BY V...

GAJA

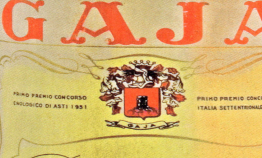

PRIMO PREMIO CONCORSO
ENOLOGICO DI ASTI 1931   PRIMO PREMIO CONCORSO
ITALIA SETTENTRIONALE 1933

Barbaresco

PREMIATA PRODUZIONE ESPORTAZIONE VINI CLASSICI
Ditta Angelo Gaja fu Giov.
ADERENTE AL CONSORZIO DIFESA VINI TIPICI DI PREGIO "BARBARESCO E BAROLO"
CASA FONDATA NEL 1859
BARBARESCO

LE CHIUSE

BAROLO
DENOMINAZIONE DI ORIGINE
CONTROLLATA E GARANTITA
2004
IMBOTTIGLIATO ALL'ORIGINE
DAL PRODUTTORE FONTANA MARIO
IN LOCALITÀ PERNO - MONFORTE D'ALBA - ITALIA
AZIENDA AGRICOLA
CASCINA FONTANA

ROSSO DI VALTELLINA
DENOMINAZIONE DI ORIGINE CONTROLLATA

NEBBIOLO
2022
ARPEPE

Piero Busso

BARBARESCO
DENOMINAZIONE DI ORIGINE CONTROLLATA E GARANTITA
GALLINA
2016
VITI VECCHIE
Sono state prodotte n°1005 bottig...
ESTATE BOTTLED BY / IMBOTTIGLIATO ALL'ORIGINE DA
SOC. AGRICOLA BUSSO S.S. DI BUSSO PIERGUIDO E BUSSO
VITICOLTORI - NEIVE - ITALIA
℮ NET CONT.750ML   ALC 14.5%...

WINE & TRAVEL
ITALY

To Mary,
an exceptional woman, mother, and sister,
an Italian who loves her roots and her family.

TEXT BY ENRICO BERNARDO

WINE & TRAVEL
ITALY

ASSOULINE

THE HARVESTING REGIONS OF ITALY

PREFACE

Since birth, Italian culture has run in my veins. While I have embarked on a mind-opening five-year trip around the world to write this series of wine and travel books, no matter where I go, my ancestral roots have given me lifelong Italian reflexes. A coffee in the morning at the counter of a bar in Naples; a Bellini on the Piazza San Marco, in Venice; a chic dinner in Milan; fried calamari on a Sardinian beach; a gelato enjoyed while out for a walk in Sicily; a pizza in Rome: these are the culinary experiences that soothed me in childhood, educated me in adolescence, and continue to expand my horizons to this day.

This is Italy, my childhood home, and still for me as an adult a favorite place to vacation, for the accents and dialects, the church towers, la dolce vita. From the elegance of its cities to the simplicity of its rural life, the Italian character is always bold. For me, the entire Italian "boot" is a land of friends, family, and a thousand years of history, during which the arts—architecture, poetry, music—have always survived even the direst wars and invasions. Italy is a land that can never lose its identity.

As is true of all the world's winegrowing countries, Italy's wines reflect its history and culture. Its winemaking traditions are richly nuanced, with thousands of small terroirs and vineyards whose varietals, appellations, and soils appear ever more colorfully varied the better you get to know them. Some of Italy's wines are legendary. A twenty-year-old Trebbiano d'Abruzzo, Fiano di Avellino, or Collio entices us with its smoky minerality. A fifty-year-old Barolo, Brunello di Montalcino, or Amarone della Valpolicella can move us deeply. And a century-old Marsala, or a passito (made from partially dried grapes) or Vin Santo ("Holy Wine") left long in the cellar, is unforgettable.

Traveling the wine routes of Italy is never in the least monotonous: each winegrowing region has its own flavors, its own light. Local specialties offer intense gustatory experiences, rich and colorful, each more appetizing than the last.

Here, then, I invite you to join me on a tour through twelve great Italian winegrowing regions, where I hope you will discover all the charming surprises that Italians know so well how to provide for their guests.

At the end of this book, you will find my list of Italy's most outstanding winemaking estates. Think of it as a chart of dreams that might come true—dreams in which each bottle finds its perfect moment through the magic of an ideal occasion or food pairing. May you share every sip in the finest company, with loved ones who understand and appreciate it as much as you do.

Enrico Bernardo
Paris

Italy is home to some of the world's most beautiful vineyards.
Following pages: Caravaggio, detail of *Bacchus*, 1598, oil on canvas, 95 x 85 cm, Uffizi Gallery, Florence.

INTRODUCTION

Italy is a land of marvels, cultural, culinary, and viticultural. Each town and stretch of countryside reveals aspects of a history stretching from antiquity to the present. This is a land blessed by all the gods, where Baroque churches may stand cheek by jowl with the ruins of ancient temples: the Forum and St. Peter's Basilica are only a few steps apart.

In Italy, to an unusual degree, the past never feels far away; it lies right before our eyes. The Colosseum in Rome or the ruins of Pompeii bring antiquity to life, just as Florence plunges us into the High Renaissance and Venice launches us on a dreamlike journey along the Silk Road. History, in its continuity and in all its layers—dazzling, magnetic, despite its moments of cruelty—is in Italy an eternal presence. It is no surprise that the country draws tens of millions of tourists from all over the world every year. Italy is universally loved.

Long divided among multiple kingdoms and duchies of varying sizes, the country was not unified until 1861, and accordingly has preserved its very powerful regional traditions. The Italian lands, however, endured numerous invasions over twenty centuries, by the Greeks, Huns, Arabs, Byzantines, Aragonese, Slavs, Savoyards, and many others. All have left traces in Italy's architecture and in its agricultural and viticultural traditions, while commercial exchanges with countries around the world have also brought innumerable cultural influences to Italian shores. The result is a mosaic spread before us astounding in its diversity. It is no exaggeration to say that every church tower corresponds to a unique dialect, accent, pasta, and local wine. In Italy, the arts of stonemasonry, food, and wine blaze forth in all their glory. And, indeed, they are connected—wherever Italy's material culture is richest, there too we invariably discover a noble winegrowing and culinary history.

The list of Italian culinary specialties, whether they come from land or sea, is one of the world's longest: antipasti, varying from one region to the next; pasta, fresh and dried, in myriad shapes; the sauces that accompany pasta, never the same twice; meats of all kinds; risottos; fish and seafood; soups; fruit and vegetables in abundance; regional specialties. Mediterranean flavors triumph across most of the Italian peninsula: aromatic herbs (basil, thyme, oregano), tomatoes, lemons, olives, eggplants. In the north, the Alpine influence is strong: horseradish, gentian, lake trout, sauced dishes, game, polenta. Sicilian tuna is exported worldwide, and the south's coastal fisheries also yield plentiful swordfish, prawns and other crustaceans, and clams.

Italy's geography is dominated by the Mediterranean and its mountain ranges, with the Alps in the north, and the Apennines, which form a spine running down the peninsula for several hundred miles. Other than some coastal strips and the plain of the Po Valley (aka the Padan Plain), flatlands are few. Since nowhere in Italy is truly arid, the landscape never presents the austere spectacle of a flat horizon. And wherever you travel, you find vineyards. Not one region is lacking in vines, for the country's multiplicity of microclimates allows a huge array of varietals to thrive on a range of soils nowhere limited to clay or sand. Moreover, each province has its indigenous varietals—perhaps there are six hundred in total in the country—organized into more than five hundred appellations.

While no varietals dominate in Italy, certain grapes have acquired a special reputation for excellence, such as Nebbiolo in Barolo and Barbaresco; Sangiovese in Montalcino and Chianti; the Nerello Mascalese grown on Mount Etna; Fiano and Greco in Irpinia; the trio of Corvina, Rondinella, and Molinara in Valpolicella; Trebbiano and Montepulciano in Abruzzo; Manduria's Primitivo; Gallura's Vermentino; another trio, this time of white-wine grapes, Collio's Friulano, Ribolla, and Malvasia; Glera in Prosecco; Aglianico in Vulture—I could go on. Such abundance, such variety—it is any wonder that the ancient Greeks nicknamed southern Italy Œnotria, "land of trained grapevines/land of wine"? Indeed, while indigenous Italian winemaking dates back to the Bronze Age (and perhaps even earlier), Greek colonists played a key role in developing Italian viticulture, beginning with their arrival in the eighth century BCE in Calabria and Sicily. The Greeks brought with them not only sophisticated winemaking methods, which eventually spread throughout the peninsula, but their own varietals, some of which are still grown in Italy today, such as Greco and Aglianico. Later, under the Roman Empire, Italian wine and winemaking know-how were exported throughout Europe.

Italy is a land of marvels, as I have said. Yet in matters culinary and viticultural, one hallmark of Italian culture is a certain modesty. Italians are endowed not only with genius and creativity but with the virtue of simplicity too. Let us not fool ourselves, however: even a seemingly easy dish like spaghetti al pomodoro is more complicated to make successfully than it looks. First, you have to choose the right tomatoes—I prefer San Marzano or Pachino. Peeling them takes skill. Next, you bring together olive oil with a bit of garlic and onion, balanced just right—not too much or too little. Add the tomatoes and season them correctly. Cook the pasta al dente, toss it in the pan to coat it with sauce. So many steps, and not obvious if you don't know how. I think too of risotto, which requires seventeen to nineteen minutes of constant stirring, depending on the variety of rice, while adding, in order: butter, shallots, rice, white wine, and ladlefuls of steaming broth (vegetable, fish, or meat stock, depending). Here's a secret: Let the risotto rest for one minute before you finally incorporate more butter and parmesan, which makes it creamy. It's easy to imagine how Paul Bocuse or the Troisgros brothers might show off their skills as they concoct such dishes, while Italian cooks maintain a modest silence—because they lack the culture of gastronomic results. In Italian eyes, it all goes back to generations-old ways of cooking handed down by la mamma. There's really no reason, I daresay, to make such a fuss about food . . .

We find the same artisanal spirit and the same reverence for inherited knowledge in Italian winegrowing. As in times past across Europe, wine in Italy symbolizes social exchange, sharing, a spiritual union of people and their land. France, to be sure, has promoted its wines with enormous success for centuries, developed elaborate regulations for classifying them, created an unequaled system for distributing them, and ensconced them on anyone's list of prestige products. Italy, by contrast, has long conceived of its wines in more workaday, less elitist terms. Concern with their promotion really dates back only to the late 1990s, when Italian wine truly entered the global market for the first time. Italian winemakers have little by little taught the wine-drinking public to differentiate the good from the better and the better from the exceptional among their offerings. (Though when it comes to food pairing, Italy has always led the way, thanks to its enormously varied cuisines.) In recent years, Italian viticulture has made great strides and brought its most outstanding wines to the fore. Today, Italian wine has even become chic—and a must on any wine list for fans worldwide. The other side of that coin, however, is the steep rise in prices among Italy's most prestigious appellations.

Please join me now, as we head off to tour Italy's finest vineyards, as rich as they are varied.

Overlooking the vineyards and castle of Castiglione Falletto. *Following pages:* A family shares some laughs while enjoying local wine, in 1983.

THE ALPS

Mont Blanc, Valtellina, and the Dolomites

The arc of Alpine peaks that rings northern Italy—a skiers' paradise—stretches from Mont Blanc and the borders with France and Switzerland in the west to the Dolomites and the Austrian border in the east. In between, in northern Lombardy's Valtellina valley, lie some of the most steeply terraced mountain vineyards on Earth. Here grow some of Italy's most treasured indigenous varietals, which seem to express the very soul of the vast surrounding forests. The alternation of hot summers and cold winters gives Italy's Alpine wines their density, while the region's wide diurnal temperature shift enables grapes to reach optimal ripeness, with thick skins rich in flavors and aromas and seeds that yield complex, silky tannins.

Alpine wines are lively, with a mouthwatering, vertical minerality. A certain uncompromising, soulful ruggedness also gives them good cut, with well-developed tannins in the reds and acidity in the whites, combining the brawniness of southern European inland terroirs with a northern directness. These are wines at once reliably structured and ample, serious, with a long finish and good balance between viscosity and freshness. When young, they offer a sharp accent on the finish, with an elegant, crystalline purity. With aging, and in particularly sunny vintages, these qualities soften and integrate—like mountain rock eroding gently over time. That directness balances on a tightrope, so complex is the alchemy among cold, fog, snow, rain, and sunshine that is one of the blessings of

A foggy sunrise over the Alpe di Siusi, in the Dolomites. *Following pages:* Overlooking the Italian Alps and local vineyards.

"All of Italy is beautiful; it's one beautiful country. In the north, we have the mountain, the acidity, and the temperature; in the south, there's the sand and another temperature. The diversity is fantastic—for both the wine and the food."

— *Matteo Furlani, winemaker, Cantina Furlani*

high elevation. In addition to their southern exposure, the considerable age of Valtellina's vines and its terraced vineyards constitutes one of the secrets of their success. These are wines that demand an intellectual approach.

Lying at the foot of Mont Blanc, the Valle d'Aosta is one of the Italian peninsula's driest regions, as the mountain chain keeps most of the rain on the French side, in Savoy and the Jura. Local dairy farmers, whose pasture-grazed cows produce the region's toma (aka tuma) cheeses, even have to irrigate their meadows. Valle d'Aosta's wines have a lot of charm and are a perfect match for winter cuisine, as vacationers know well—hence the high level of consumption in the skiing season, which unfortunately restricts the wines' wider distribution. The valley's cépages are of varied character. Among the whites, the aromatic Petite Arvine, very sapid Blanc de Morgex, perfumed Muscat de Chambave, and mineral Chardonnay are all distinctive. As for reds, wines made from Fumin are very tasty—spicy, even peppery—while those made from Petit Rouge are rather fruity and light.

A Petite Arvine accompanied by white asparagus with mint-infused extra-virgin olive oil makes for a marvelous union of intense flavors and tender textures. The Grosjean brothers' Vigne Rovettaz is a magnificent example. Other delightful estates include Les Crêtes, whose magnificent Chardonnays age well; Anselmet, with its excellent Pinot Nero (the Italian name for Pinot Noir); and Ermes Pavese, whose very light and crystalline Blanc de Morgex pairs well with raw oysters.

In Valtellina, near the Swiss border, the soils have little clay but plenty of mineral-rich sands resulting from slow erosion of rock. With its spectacular vineyards, which appear to be suspended between the valley and the sky (and are located to maximize solar exposure), the region is the symbol of viticultural heroism. Each of the valley's top crus—in the Sassella, Grumello, Valgella, and Inferno subzones—in its own way incarnates the rugged elegance of the Chiavennasca grape, the "Nebbiolo of Piedmont." Valtellina also includes the Sforzato (aka Sfursat) di Valtellina DOCG, whose powerful wine is produced by the appassimento process (air-drying of the grapes on straw mats for three months, a method thought to have been originally developed in Greece to concentrate grape sugar). Sforzato is perfect with pizzoccheri, a local specialty made with a traditional buckwheat pasta boiled with potatoes and a bit of green cabbage, all then baked with butter and the local toma to create a light gratiné: the dish's creaminess marries perfectly with the wine's astringent tannins. A Grumello Rocca de Piro from Ar.Pe.Pe would also be a fine

A lot of international grapes, such as Cabernet Sauvignon and Merlot, have been grown in the Alto Adige vineyards, making some of the world's best wine.

match. This estate, in my view, epitomizes the region's extremely challenging form of viticulture, which requires annual reconstruction of the low stone walls that hold the terraces together. I have happily savored Grumello's 2016 Riserva, which unites subtlety and depth and all the linearity of its mountainous terroir with almost fragile notes of dried roses, cherry preserves, black pepper, a hint of truffle, and a long, persistent finish. Drinking such a wine is a truly elevating experience!

The Dolomites form a magnificent range of mountains within the Italian Alps, and are included on UNESCO's World Heritage List. They are of rare beauty, in both summer and winter, when their slopes offer exceptionally fine skiing. I love the purity of this region's wines: the whites are crystalline, and the reds luscious—with an Austrian accent. Austria's proximity explains why, alongside the very successful Chardonnay, Sauvignon Blanc (in Italy usually called simply Sauvignon), and Pinot Nero, it is not unusual to find Riesling, Muller-Thürgau, Sylvaner, Kerner, Pinot Bianco (Pinot Blanc), Pinot Grigio (Pinot Gris), and Traminer among the white cépages, and Schiava (aka Trollinger and Vernatsch) and Lagrein among the reds. Grown on highly mineral soils, all these grapes reveal a lightly sapid aspect here. Top producers include Cantina Terlano, Gump Hof, Köfererhof, and Taschlerhof. I particularly remember a twenty-year-old Chardonnay from Cantina Terlano whose salinity and minerality simply sparkled.

Near the town of Trento lies Maso Martis, a real gem of an estate, led today by Giulio Ferrari and long recognized for the quality of its sparkling wines. But the Trento region also produces delicious reds based on Teroldego and/or Cabernet Sauvignon that marry to perfection with a creamy polenta or sauced meat dishes. The Foradori and Tenuta San Leonardo estates, offering two very different styles, are both good ambassadors for the region. One rare local specialty is a Vin Santo made from Nosiola—like Sforzato, a wine made by air-drying grapes on straw mats for several months. The result is a sweet wine magnificent with an aged Alpine cheese.

Slow morning outside Johnson & Dipoli, in Egna. *Opposite:* A moment of calm to savor some locally produced wine.

"Great wines are born in the vineyards. In the cellars, the most we can do is bring out our grape's best qualities. That means our legacy is in this soil."

— Maurizio Zanella, winegrower, Ca' Del Bosco

"Three things matter when you choose a wine: territory, the weather of that specific production year, and the winemakers."

— Max Niccoli, Italian wine expert

The lush greenery of Northern Italy, cared for by all the local winegrowers.
Following pages: Picking some edible flowers from the garden to garnish a homemade meal.

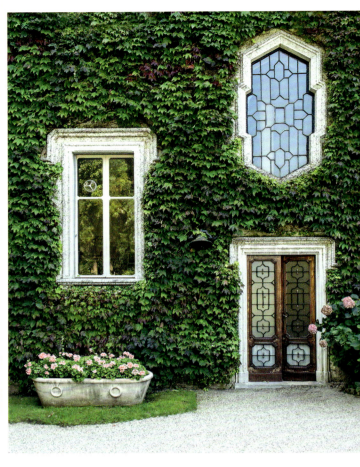

"In northern Lombardy's Valtellina valley, lie some of the most steeply terraced mountain vineyards on Earth."

— Enrico Bernardo

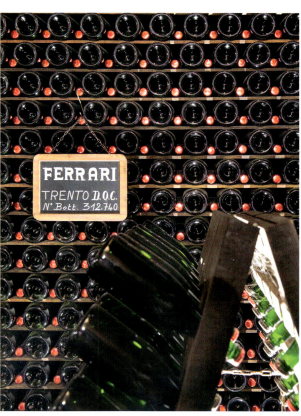

Traditions and tried-and-true local dishes make for the most remarkable journey through the Italian Alps. *Previous pages, from left:* The cloister at the Neustift Abbey (or Abbazia di Novacella), in Vahrn, once served as a medieval corridor linking the abbey church, dining hall, and dormitory; setting the table before service begins. *Following pages:* Engraving from 1926 depicting a wine tasting in the heart of the Italian Alps.

Wine growing is passed down from generation to generation.
Following pages: The beauty of Lake Braies, in the Trentino-Alto Adige region.

THE ADRIATIC COAST

From Bologna to Abruzzo

The winegrowing areas of Italy's central Adriatic Coast lie opposite Croatia. Here, the Adriatic Sea is not very deep, and the coastal lands are mostly flat. Intense summer heat offers winegrowers the advantage of high vineyard yields. The area's highest-quality wines tend to come from gently sloping sites lying just a few miles from shore, though in some areas, fine vineyards are also found in cooler valleys farther inland, such as the Valle Reale in Abruzzo. The climate of such estates is much more mountain than maritime, for lofty peaks are seldom far away. Gran Sasso and Maiella, both in Abruzzo, for example, reach nearly 3,000 meters/9,850 feet high. As we travel north to south along the coast, we pass through three wine regions: Emilia-Romagna, centered around the city of Bologna; Marche (sometimes in English called "the Marches" or that name's Italian equivalent, "le Marche"); and Abruzzo.

In Romagna, we can hardly avoid Lambrusco, the sparkling red everyone knows—a simple wine, sometimes mass-produced. Still, some Lambrusco estates, such as Cantina Paltrinieri, strive to maintain high quality, highlighting the wine's effervescence, freshness, and simplicity, which makes it a marvelous match for many dishes, from those with rich, savory sauces to cheeses such as a great parmigiano to fresh pastas—ravioli, tortellini, lasagna—or prosciutto di Parma. I particularly recommend three appellations: Lambrusco di Sorbara, Lambrusco Grasparossa di Castelvetro, and Lambrusco Salamino di Santa Croce. Still in Romagna, we may enjoy a wine made from the Albana varietal, either dry (with, say, a fish

"Today, young people prefer lighter wines and are very attentive to the communication of the company, to which we give a lot of importance, from the label we use for our wines to social media."

— Alessandra Quarta, winegrower, Claudio Quarta Vignaiolo

"Making everything by hand is not only a respect for tradition—we are still making wine the same way people were doing it a hundred years ago in Abruzzo—but because the result is consistently different."

— Chiara De Iulis Pepe, winegrower, Emidio Pepe

soup) or sweet (perhaps with saffron biscotti, as an afternoon refreshment). In Emilia, the area between Bologna and Piacenza includes the Gutturnio DOC for white and several simple reds made from Barbera and Croatina, some lightly sparkling, all fine accompaniments to a spread of antipasti misti including gnocco fritto (Emilian fried dough) with mortadella.

Marche offers wines with bold personalities due to its often poor soils and wide diurnal temperature shift. Whites from Verdicchio grown in the DOCs of Castelli di Jesi (especially Villa Bucci's, a must) and Matelica (especially Bisci's, another must) are delicious: subtle, mouthwatering, perfect with shellfish and other seafood. Fattoria San Lorenzo's Verdicchios are also absolutely not to be missed. This third-generation family estate, since 1995 in the hands of Natalino Crognaletti, offers several luminous whites that achieve a plateau of marvelous complexity after seven or eight years' aging.

Also worth seeking out are wines from the Bianchello del Metauro DOC, made from Bianchello (aka Biancame) which, like Marche whites made from Trebbiano, Pecorino, or Passerina, are ideal with local fish and vegetables grown on farms inland, richly aromatic and appetizing. Rounding out the picture are the reds of the Rosso Conero, Rosso Piceno, and Vernaccia di Serrapetrona appellations. Conero and Piceno, both based on Montepulciano, are lusciously expressive, lovely with grilled meats. Vernaccia, a sparkler, is a cool, thirst-quenching aperitif in its secco version or a fine dessert wine accompanying red berries when off-dry or sweet. In the province of Ancona, the dry, food-friendly reds of the Lacrima di Morro d'Alba DOC reveal unusually floral notes, especially rose—nice with, say, a spicy tuna tartare.

Arriving in Abruzzo, we find ourselves in one of the finest and most exciting of Italy's wine regions. There are two major appellations: Trebbiano d'Abruzzo and Montepulciano d'Abruzzo. The former is a slightly astringent white, chewy and drying on the tongue. With age, these Trebbianos develop great aromatic complexity and substance, with notes of spices, stone fruits, and gentian. The result is truly mouthwatering and well-suited to a richly flavored and varied cuisine. I recall a 1985 Valentini, a truly monumental wine, that could have passed for a grand cru white Burgundy in a blind tasting, with its complex panoply of flavors, its purity and length. All by itself, it was extraordinary, but it would have been marvelous accompanying a roast guinea fowl with the season's first cèpes. As for Montepulciano d'Abruzzo, it can be a special thrill when grown on poor soils in a cool terroir, when it offers great elegance, young or old. In addition, again, to Valentini, I have fine memories of cuvées from Valle Reale, Nicoletta de Fermo, and Emidio Pepe, among many others.

Wine tasting with friends at Claudio Quarta Vignaiolo.

From Alberobello to Locorotondo, soaking in the Italian sun.

"We have revolutionized communication, while remaining true to our history and tradition. A revolution that has shifted the focus from product to people."

— Marianna Velenosi, winegrower, Cantina Velenosi

"My passion for wine is a heritage coming from the emotional farmer making wines for himself, for the family and the few guys worthy of his friendship."

— *Massimo Palmieri, winegrower, Tenuta San Marcello*

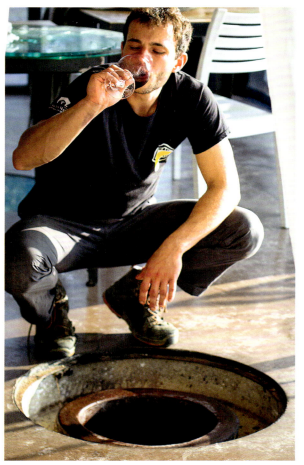

Sampling products and harvesting grapes on the Adriatic coast. *Following pages, from left:* Sailing on the Adriatic Riviera, circa 1960; a UNESCO World Heritage site, Alberobello is full of dwellings made of dry stones and conical roofs covered with limestone lauzes.

"*Back in the day, this area was all covered by water, so the soils are full of salt and minerals because of the sea.*"

— *Chiara De Iulis Pepe, winegrower, Emidio Pepe*

Fishing, sailing, and tasting delicious local dishes in Puglia.
Previous pages: By the sea on San Nicola di Tremiti Island.

"Here, the Adriatic Sea is not very deep, the coastal lands are mostly flat, and the intense summer heat offers winegrowers the advantage of high vineyard yields."

— Enrico Bernardo

Colorful details and produce in the streets of Puglia and Salento. *Following pages, from left:* Stopping for a lunch under the Italian sun; lunchtime with local bread and some charcuterie in Le Marche.

"The harvest takes place exclusively by hand and the crushing takes place within one hour of harvesting. This allows us to be able to work with intact and perfectly healthy grapes."

— Fabrizio Palmieri, winegrower, Tenuta San Marcella

Celebratory moments in traditional Italian costumes.
Previous pages, from left: Overlooking the crystal blue waters and cliffs of Isla de San Domino; the Lecce Cathedral, in the heart of Apulia.

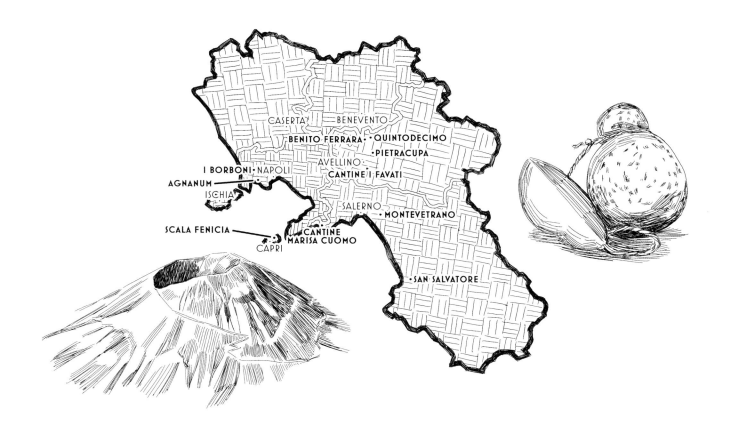

THE AMALFI COAST

Naples, Sorrento, and Capri

With magnificent destinations such as Naples, Pompeii, Capri, Ischia, Sorrento, Positano, and the Royal Palace of Caserta, Italy's Amalfi Coast is a must for cultural tourists and wine lovers both. We all have a mental picture postcard of an idealized, timeless southern Italy: chic and elegant, painted in lemon yellow, sweet-basil green, and tomato red, all set against the sunny blue skies of spring or late summer. We might not spontaneously associate wine with that image, yet the region's wines are not only legion but of high quality too. As I note in the introduction above, many aspects of this region's viticulture trace back to the Greeks, especially red varietals like Aglianico and whites like Greco. Others have been cultivated for some two thousand years, like the white cépages Falanghina and Biancolella and the red Piedirosso. During the Roman Empire, Campania developed greatly. With Pompeii as its most important commercial center, and thanks to port towns like Pozzuoli, massive quantities of wine were exported to other Mediterranean countries, including France.

To explore the narrow alleys of Naples, stopping at random to savor an espresso in the morning accompanied by a babà al rum or a sfogliatella (a pastry stuffed with ricotta and candied orange zest and flavored with vanilla or cinnamon)—there is no better way to wake up the mind, and the tastebuds. And sitting down in the evening with friends to enjoy a pizza washed down with a lively bottle of sparkling Asprinio d'Aversa is quite simply life the

"The branches of the vines clinging to the large trees would be said to be many triumphal arches prepared for the passage of a powerful monarch."

— Aubert de Linsolas

From boat rides to homemade dishes by the sea, the Amalfi Coast has many wonders to offer.

way it is meant to be lived. An excursion to see Pompeii or climb the slopes of Vesuvius helps you to understand how even very simple wines, like a Campi Flegrei or a Vesuvio Lacryma Christi hold a well-deserved place in the varied panorama of Campanian winegrowing. By the way, the name Lacryma Christi ("Christ's tears") comes from a legend according to which Jesus, while wandering the earth, one day found himself at the mountain's foot. Enthralled by the beauty of the place, he concluded that Lucifer must have pulled a little piece of Heaven down with him when he fell. Deeply moved, Jesus wept. Some local women who witnessed the scene decided to plant grapevines on the very spot.

A few minutes' drive inland, east of Naples, near the town of Avellino, lies one of the loveliest places for winegrowing in all of Italy, Irpinia, which includes four great DOCGs: two white, Fiano di Avellino and Greco di Tufo; and two red, Taurasi and Aglianico del Taburno. Both whites grow on tufa soils that soak up spring rain to sustain the vines during hot, dry periods. These are expressive wines, linear and sapid, with notes of citrus and gunflint. The Greco has a rounder, fruitier profile. Benito Ferrara's "Vigna Cicogna" Greco di Tufo is remarkable. The Fiano grape resembles the kind of varietals high in sugar that attract honeybees. There is a very real difference between these two white grapes: with aging, Fiano takes on mineral and gunflint flavors that can be reminiscent of grand cru Chablis, while Greco gains in fruit and amplitude. Both wines marry marvelously well with the rich Neapolitan cuisine, including ocean fish; all the fine local agricultural products, especially citrus fruit; and the exceptional Gragnano durum wheat, used to make some of Italy's finest pastas (dry Gragnano pasta is renowned for its extraordinary keeping quality too), perfect with seafood. Greco is a fine match for octopus, calamari, and strongly flavored vegetables such as artichoke, eggplant, or peppers, while Fiano is good with sea urchins, mussels, and fish baked with zucchini and onion confit. Pietracupa's Fiano, with fifteen years' aging, somehow reminds me of a great Italian soprano; it is a wine pure, long, and complex, with notes of iodine and smoke. The Irpinian reds, with their warmth and tannic structure, are ideal with meat or pasta in sauce, so long as garlic, onions, and tomatoes are never too far away. Wines from all four of these appellations benefit with long aging, which lends them a thrillingly rich bouquet.

Campania is a region of ancient viticultural traditions. About half of its land is hilly, and one-third mountainous, with a great variety not only of soils (volcanic, tufa, chalk/limestone) but also of microclimates, given that the sea is never far off. Campania's Aversa Asprinio DOC is special. Here, the slightly acidic Asprinio grape struggles to get enough sun to achieve optimal ripeness. So for centuries, local winegrowers have relied on a trellising technique called vite maritata, believed

Savoring mussels by the beach at Da Adolfo.

to date back to the ancient Etruscans, in which grapevines are encouraged to grow skyward by climbing, like lianas, up the trunks of trees planted in the vineyards—a true marriage of branch and vine. Though harvesttime requires high ladders, the system works: as early as the fourteenth century, Asprinio was recognized for the quality of its sparkling wines. Today, the I Borboni estate in particular maintains this tradition with brio.

The fertile lands of Cilento, in southern Campania, yield red wines of high quality. Here, the Montevetrano estate, with its blends of Cabernet Sauvignon, Aglianico, and Merlot, is incontestably great. These lush wines are perfect with Gragnano fusilli in a lightly spiced tomato sauce.

Finally, I would be remiss if I neglect to mention the Amalfi Coast and the Sorrento Peninsula. Beyond its landscapes' breathtaking beauty, this region offers light, tasty wines with a marine note, like those produced by Cantina Marisa Cuomo, made with indigenous grapes such as Biancolella and Falanghina—equally sublime with sea bream carpaccio in olive oil and lemon, enjoyed on a terrace in Capri, or with calamari fritti in Ischia.

Italian writer and journalist Curzio Malaparte at a restaurant by the sea in Capri, circa 1920s. *Opposite:* Soaking in the sun before a boat ride.

"This is the promised land; in the countryside you see festoons of vines attached to the trees with scattered bunches of grapes."

— Carolina Bonaparte, about the land of Asprinio

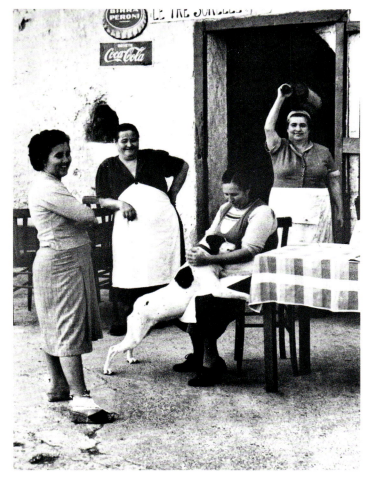

Nostalgic moments on the Amalfi Coast, a summer destination for many decades.
Following pages, from left: Fresh tomatoes to be savored on their own, or in unique Italian recipes; harvesting grapes at Cantine Bonaparte.

Vibrant moments by the water.

"Many aspects of this region's viticulture trace back to the Greeks, especially red varietals like Aglianica and whites like Greca. Others have been cultivated for some two thousand years." — Enrica Bernado

"The vines that climb the slopes of Vesuvius have come down to us directly from the Aminei, an ancient people of the northern Greek region of Thessaly, who brought the vines when they arrived in this area in the fifth century BC."

— Maurizio Russi, winegrower, Cantina del Vesuvio

From harvesting grapes to tasting local wines, Italian vineyards are home to unique experiences. *Following pages, from left:* Hand-painted ceramics make for the perfect souvenir of time spent on the Amalfi Coast; ceramic tile artwork of fishermen around Amalfi.

Many vineyards on the Amalfi Coast provide visitors with bespoke experiences to immerse themselves in local winemaking.

"The selection of noble grapes, the search for the right degree of freshness and humidity, combined with the passage of time, old secrets handed down by the local winemakers and the advanced technology used by today's technicians give life to wines of the finest quality, appreciated the world over."

— Andrea Ferraioli and Marisa Cuomo, winegrowers, Cantine Marisa Cuomo

SICILY

Volcanic and Island Flavors

It is impossible not to fall in love with Sicily. The island is so rich, so varied, that it could be an entire country all by itself. Sicily's past is fascinating, as its lovely towns and cities testify: Palermo, rough around the edges yet majestic; Taormina, a hilltop jewel amid superb coastal landscapes; Noto, a Baroque pearl; Agrigento, with its vast Valley of the Temples; and of course Syracuse. Sicilians today consider themselves to be purely Italian, and have never felt tempted by separatism since Italy's unification in 1861. Their pride, rooted in the island's geography as much as its history, transcends provincialism. Sicilians are endowed with a natural nobility; they trust that promises made are promises kept. Another indication of the islanders' values is the royal treatment they accord to grandparents and children—to me a sign of generosity and the beauty of the Sicilian soul. And if you run a restaurant, as I have, you are always delighted to have Sicilians as customers.

The island's coastal cuisine, as you would expect, revolves around its fisheries, featuring prawns, swordfish (often served raw, alla carpaccio), and tuna—of which Sicily is a major exporter, whose tuna today is popular worldwide. In addition to these fine products, we must add octopus, dried fish, calamari, anchovies, sardines, and sea bream—all prepared in every imaginable way. The inland cookery relies heavily on a blend of salty, savory, "dry" flavors—oregano, capers, olives, almonds, pistachios—which give everyday dining a very specific tonality.

An eighteenth-century aristocratic villa, Monaci delle Terre Nere is a one-of-a-kind place inspired by Sicilian nature.
Following pages, from left: Pausing for some handmade pizza on a hot summer day; colorful hand-painted boats in Taormina.

I cherish wonderful memories of Sicily. One May, while scootering around the Aeolian Islands off Sicily's northeastern coast, I recall being stopped by a gust of chamomile—a wild perfume emanating from a nook between the road and the sea. Another time, in a harbor café where I was drinking my morning coffee, I watched the unloading of an freshly caught swordfish. The fishermen cut me a fine slice of the flesh to eat raw: what a marvelous way to start the day in Sicily!

A little like Piedmont, Sicily produces many different kinds of wine. And I must list them all, not for the sake of inclusiveness per se, but because they all deserve attention. Vineyards in the north, around Mount Etna, the region's standard-bearer, offer many single-parcel reds with strong varietal character and pure, clean flavors. This is one of the most beautiful places imaginable for winegrowing. Etna's estates are called contrade (literally, "lands"), with vines that can be over a century old growing in vast, often terraced vineyards, braced and surrounded by low walls made of volcanic stone. It is quite a sight—the vines' green leaves and bright fruit set off against the black earth. The Etna DOC's terroir is under 1,000 hectares/2,470 acres, divided into small vineyard parcels, yet its small production does not prevent Etna wines from being known and sought worldwide. The reds are lean and graceful, but full of energy, with seductive notes of bitter orange, gooseberry, blueberry, and dried herbs. I recall enjoying a bottle of Profumo di Vulcano from Federico Graziani, a former sommelier who shifted to winegrowing—an unusual career change, in his case crowned with success. This cuvée deserves its name, which means "scent of the volcano." To taste it is an explosive experience—this is a vertical wine positively trembling with fire. The Profumo would be a perfect match for a roasted fillet of tuna with confit of peppers, or for red meat in sauce. Other Etna domains that will sweep you off your feet include Benanti, Girolamo Russo, Graci Vigneri di Salvo Foti, Passopisciaro, and Graci Vigneri di Salvo Foti.

Sicily also produces dry whites, saline and mineral, made from Grillo. Grillo is also blended with such other Sicilian varietals as Inzolia and Catarratto to make Marsala, one of the world's finest oxidative-style wines, which can age well for over a century. Marsala is delicious with a well-aged parmigiano or a black-pepper-speckled pecorino. Marco de Bartoli's oldest Marsalas, with their very persistent finish, are wines to savor meditatively.

Alongside these dry and oxidative styles, we also find great liqueurs, such as those made on the island of Pantelleria from Moscatto (Muscat), and on Lipari from Malvasia. Both offer a good balance among sweetness, fruitiness, and salinity, and are nice enjoyed with biscotti or almond cakes, or simply with ice cream or ricotta-filled cannoli with confit fruit. These wines may be rather over the top when young, but they gain in real amplitude with time; their aromatic complexity and very persistent finish are always key.

In Vittoria, near Syracuse, we find reds that are floral, fruity, and light, but never bland, made from Frappato, with its strawberry-scented nose, and from Nero d'Avola, scented with violets. They are terrific with stuffed tomatoes, tuna carpaccio, or a fillet of red mullet fresh out of the sea. In central Sicily, Nero d'Avola yields headier reds, richer and more robust, which have gained an international following. Meanwhile, between Syracuse and Ragusa, near the city of Noto, renowned for its Baroque architecture, we find sweet Moscattos of incredible charm. Finally, to close this long list—and let me say again, Sicily is one of Italy's greatest wine regions—we also find a few interesting sparklers here too.

The crystal waters around Levanzo Island.
Following pages, from left: Playful nights at Animaetnea Winery; walking on the Stair of the Turks rock cliff, near Porto Empedocle.

Colorful tiles meet bold graphics in the streets of Sicily. *Previous pages:* Traditional wine cart drawn by a donkey in Palermo. *Following pages, from left:* Locally made charcuterie in Syracuse; the streets of Sicily, set in time.

"In managing the cellar, tradition will always be the fulcrum of our essence, a tradition that has been handed down to us and of which we are the heirs."

— *Federica Fina, winegrower, Cantina Fina*

"*Donnafugata white wines, with a strong Mediterranean soul, stand out for their freshness, distinctive minerality and their aromatic structure.*"

— *Giacomo Rallo, winegrower, Donnafugata*

Happy memories from the 1960s, including at Dimora Delle Balze (opposite). *Following pages, from left:* Villa Elena, restored and designed by Jacques Garcia, was more recently used as a film location for the *White Lotus* series; the Donnafugata winery is known for its small, prestigious productions from unique estates and vineyards. *Pages 104-05:* Hiding from the Sicilian sun in this grand patio.

"It is impossible not to fall in love with Sicily. The island is so rich, so varied, that it could be an entire country all by itself."

— Enrico Bernardo

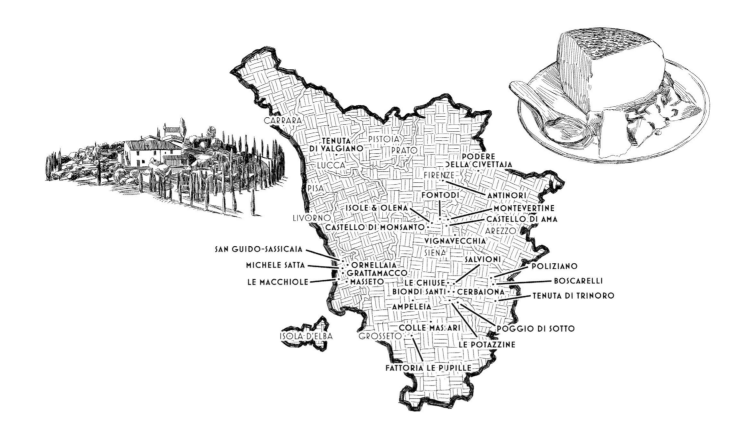

TUSCANY

———————◆———————

Florence, Siena, Chianti, and Brunello di Montalcino

In Tuscany we plunge into another great Italian winegrowing region, also one of the most popular of the country's tourist destinations. Like the Amalfi Coast, Tuscany also offers magnificent postcard scenery: the gently rolling golden hills, cypress-lined lanes leading to ancient farmsteads, olive groves with glimmering gray-green foliage. With Florence as its capital, among so many other illustrious cities—Siena, Pisa, Luca, Livorno—Tuscany is the birthplace of the Renaissance, of poets, sculptors, and writers whose light spread anew throughout Italy as the Middle Ages waned. Tuscany is a region long dominated by an aristocratic class of barons and marquises whose families built vast rural estates over many generations where peasant farmers grew grapes, grains, and olives. Yet the tide of history eventually turned, and the great Tuscan estates were more or less abandoned, as they were throughout Italy in the early modern era. In the 1960s, the Tuscan government sought to attract farmers from other regions, above all Marche, to restore the region's agriculture. Around the hill town of Montalcino, in the province of Siena, land was even given away for free—land that today includes the famed Brunello vineyards and is worth a fortune.

Surprisingly, the cuisine of this land blessed by the gods relies on simple foodstuffs. Signature Tuscan dishes, for example, include pappa al pomodoro, a soup served warm or cool made from tomatoes, garlic, basil, stale bread, and peppers; or bistecca alla fiorentina, a T-bone steak charcoal-grilled with olive oil and ground pepper—it can be

Overlooking the surrounding vineyards from a Tuscan villa.
Following pages: One of the most prolific wine-producing regions in Europe, Tuscany is known for Sangiovese-based dry red wines.

excellent, but the preparation is not really unusual. Tuscan bread is unsalted, and many recipes make use of day-old slices, for example cacciucco, a fish soup from Livorno, or ribollita, a thick potage made with beans, cabbage, and other inexpensive vegetables. Local game, legumes, cheeses, and charcuterie complete the picture.

Tuscany complements its simple cuisine with an array of extraordinary wines grown in one of Italy's driest and sunniest terroirs. Brunello di Montalcino, the queen of them all, is generous, fleshy, and structured, and demands long aging in foudres. The greatest Brunellos, to my taste, are Salvioni's and Le Chiuse's Riserva Diecianni, both charming wines with extraordinary density and volume. They are best enjoyed with a Tuscan pasta, the thick hand-rolled rustic spaghetti called pici (or pinci in Montalcino), dressed with a rich game ragù—and followed by a royal siesta. Montalcino's cépage is Sangiovese Grosso, which has thicker skin than Chianti's Sangiovese, but with great aromatic intensity and aging potential. Brunello has for many years enjoyed enormous success in the United States, where it has become perhaps Italy's best-known red wine. American wine drinkers love Brunellos' richness, density, structure, and high ABV (up to 15%, and sometimes higher). Regulations require a Brunello to age at least five years, six for a riserva (with two years on oak for both), and to be sold no earlier than January 1 of the sixth year following harvest.

Tuscany's other flagship wine is Chianti, which has enjoyed great fame for much longer, since its production goes back to the thirteenth century. There are two DOCGs here: Chianti Classico and Chianti. The former remains faithful to its historical origins, and grows in villages whose elevation attenuates summer heat. The gallo nero, a black rooster in silhouette on the bottle's capsule, identifies a Classico. I recall tasting many vintages of Fontodi's Flaccianello della Pieve, Castello di Monsanto's Il Poggio Riserva, and Montevertine's Le Pergole Torte, discovering in each a wine that never ceases to become more refined as the years pass. Il Poggio Riserva is in fact grown outside Chianti's historic zone, and its quality is highly variable, ranging from merely basic to a subtlety that rivals the finest bottles. In the traditional Chianti terroir, between Siena and Florence, by contrast, the prevalence of forested areas enhances the annual rainfall, which results

Improvised picnic on the grounds of winery Tenuta Dodici,
which spans more than thirteen hectares of vineyards.

"Tuscany is the first thing that comes to mind thanks to Florence, Siena, and their rich cultural and historical traditions."

— Franco Ziliani, Italian wine expert

Peaceful moments spent recharging and taking in the Tuscan sun.

in elegant wines with higher acidity and riper tannins. The wines grown here are sober, elegant, fruity, and delicate; they marry very well with poultry or veal dishes. They can even be served lightly chilled to preserve their crushed-red-fruit character. A third Sangiovese DOCG, lying further south, toward Arezzo, bears the name Vino Nobile di Montepulciano, whose wines are sunnier, denser, and also highly successful on the international market.

Bolgheri, a fourth, and very unusual, Tuscan red appellation, demands some background explanation. In southern Tuscany, in the 1960s, on a low-lying family estate by the sea, Marquis Nicolò Incisa della Rocchetta began working with his father, Mario. Father and son, both admirers of great Bordeaux like Château Latour and Château Margaux, seeking to make wine according to their own taste, decided to grow Cabernet Sauvignon and Merlot on their estate's gravel soils. Without the support of any appellation, their products had for many years to be sold as table wines prior to being officially recognized with the founding of the Bolgheri appellation. Yet the winemakers' defiance of norms and their uncommon creativity enabled some of their releases to achieve an unprecedented level of excellence, heedless of all that the established appellations imposed. Ultimately, the della Rochettas would produce the first Italian wine to meet with comparable success on the global market, and today one of the country's most admired and best-known wines of all: Sassicaia. And so were born the Super Tuscans, constituting a whole new, freely inventive school of Italian winemaking that has since influenced other regions in Italy and outside it, from Spain to southern France to Greece and beyond.

Even so, we are hardly done with Tuscany, a veritable wine lover's paradise, where high quality is today the cardinal virtue. Continuing further south, we come to the Morellino di Scansano DOCG in Maremma, whose Sangioveses are fresh and fruity. The Bianco di Pitigliano DOC, lying a bit inland from the coast opposite the island of Elba, is bracing alongside grilled prawns or calamari. A bit to the north we find the Vernaccia di San Gimignano DOCG, whose whites are sapid and lightly astringent, with notes of almond and freshly cut grass, a fine match for razor clams simply dressed with butter and salt. Still another famed regional specialty is Vin Santo, which benefits here from long aging, first in oak, then in bottle. Tuscan Vin Santo is legendary; Tuscans themselves even allow their children to dunk biscotti in the sweet wine as a treat.

In northern Tuscany, near the border with Liguria, we find white wines made from Vermentino that have a sunny character and notes of citrus mingled with aromatic herbs. And finally, there are the hillside vineyards near Lucca, where splendid wines have been made since ancient times. Today, this subregion grows a wide range of cépages, including Syrah, Merlot, and Sangiovese among the reds, and Sémillon, Roussanne, Trebbiano, Viognier, Vermentino, and Grechetto among whites.

Exploring the Tuscan terroir. *Following pages:* Taking in every moment of rest and fun at Cantina Salcheto, a sustainable winery that produces organic and natural wine.

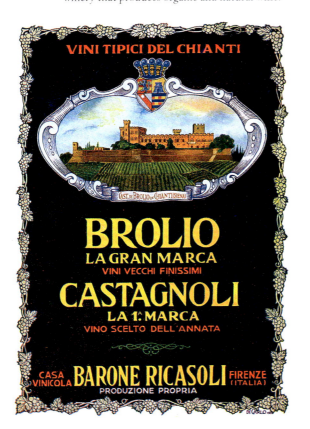

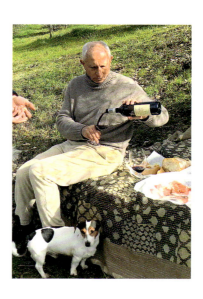

"The best wine is the one that is balanced in everything. This means fruity notes, tannins, elegance; the best wines of Tuscany have all these factors."

— Franco Ziliani, Italian wine expert

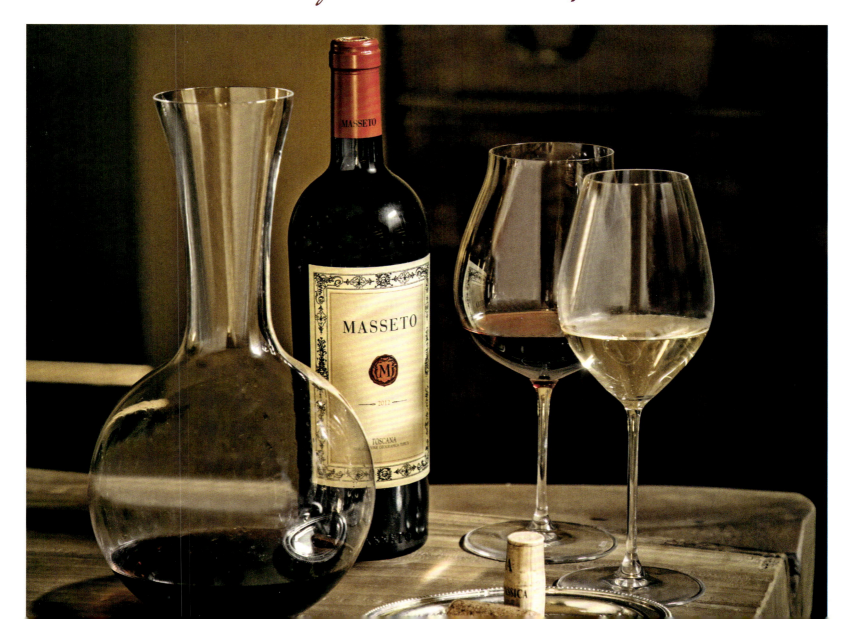

«Quando la mente s'innalza al di sopra dei nomi e delle forme, non pensa che toccare il punto in cui anche le divisioni sessuali vengono superate»

«La soggettività è un liquido sommovimento, non tollera definizioni che siano altro dai fervidi le risoluzioni io sento che si amori più fervidi le risoluzioni più tragiche ritardano le nomenclature e le opere condannano a via durano sul a più pochi decenni più eminenti si compiono in silenzio, ineffabilmente»

Elémire Zolla

Candid moments while sampling products in Tuscany.
Following pages, from left: Harvesting at Winery Tenuta Dodici; pasta and mussels make for a delicious, homemade meal.

"We are in a unique territory for Sangiovese, that is called Conca d'oro, or 'gold basin,' for a reason."

— Dario Faccin, winegrower, Tenuta Carobbio

Harvesting grapes in the Chianti Hills near Florence, before enjoying a cheese and charcuterie board under the sun. *Following pages, from left:* The vineyards around Rosewood Castiglion del Bosco, a luxury hotel within one of the oldest estates in Tuscany; mindful, sustainable practices have made Ruffino's legacy for more than 140 years.

"The premises of the production zone are embedded in the hill, which allows to maintain temperature and humidity at a stable level throughout the year."

— Angelo Migliori, winegrower, Tenuta Dodici

Wine tasting and celebrations over the decades, including at Antinori nel Chanti Classico, which provides a multidisciplinary experience in enology (*opposite*).

"Tuscany complements its simple cuisine with an array of extraordinary wines grown in one of Italy's driest and sunniest terroirs."

— Enrico Bernardo

THE VENETO

From Verona to Venice

    The Veneto is at once an industrial region and heavily touristed—unusual in Italy. However, when we invoke the names of Verona or Venice, it is not industrial enterprises that come to mind but rather the country's most prestigious theaters, the Verona Arena and Venice's La Fenice. Venice, one of the most visited cities on Earth, is much more, of course: the grandeur of an independent republic led by the doges for a thousand years, a city that fused the majesty of Italian Catholicism with a culture of intense artistic creativity and an all-powerful commercial empire more closely connected to the East than any other European capital.

    When it comes to wine, the Veneto has much to be proud of. East of Verona there reigns a famous red, Valpolicella, one of Italy's simplest and tastiest wines, made from a blend of three indigenous varietals, Corvina, Rondinella, and Molinara. Pale in color, lightly fruity, a pretty, cheerful, unpretentious Italian wine, Valpolicella has no equal when paired with a plate of ham, barbecued meat, pizza, pasta in tomato sauce, or even a simple ham-and-mozzarella sandwich. While Valpolicella drinks like a Beaujolais, I also compare its image and style to Bardolino, whose terroir lies closer to Lake Garda.

    By contrast, the Veneto also produces one of Italy's most highly structured wines, Amarone, and one of its most complex, Recioto. The latter, despite being simply splendid, is going through a difficult period, like many other similar

wines around the world that are out of fashion because they are viscous and sweet. Like Vin Santo, Recioto is made from grapes air-dried for several months (traditionally on straw mats) to concentrate their sugar. An exceptional wine that can age well for a century, Recioto presents concentrated sweet flavors of prune, fig, and mulberry, but also a lovely acidity, and with freshness on the finish. Tasting a thirty-six-month-aged parmigiano accented with a few drops of thirty-year-old balsamic vinegar alongside a glass of this nectar will send you straight to seventh heaven. For sheer intensity, complexity, and persistence of flavors and aromas, there is no equal. Giuseppe Quintarelli's Recioto is equally a masterpiece accompanying a chocolate dessert.

As for Amarone, its production is steadily increasing to satisfy high demand, especially in the U.S. This red is made with the same technique as Recioto, but with a shorter period of air drying of the fruit, yielding powerful dry cuvées. Nonetheless, Amarones are sufficiently concentrated to reach a high ABV—typically 15% or more—which makes them attractive to neophyte drinkers. Traditionally, Amarone has been considered to be perfect in and with game dishes like lièvre à la royale (whole hare braised in red

Evening wine tasting. *Opposite:* Nightlife in a Vicenza piazza, dominated by the sixteenth-century Basilica Palladiana.

wine and served with a sauce that includes its heart, liver, lungs, and blood)—that is, confined within a rather narrow culinary register. Yet the wine's roundness and density have proven so pleasing that for several years now it has won over drinkers in Asia, especially China, where it is surely drunk with dishes other than game. One result of Amarone's massive output today is that we must choose carefully among its producers. I recommend Giuseppe Quintarelli, Roccolo Grassi, Ca' La Bionda, Bussola Tommaso, and older vintages from Bertani.

Regarding Bertani, I cherish a special memory of one of his older vintages that still moves me. This was in Verona—Romeo and Juliet's home town—during Vinitaly, the annual Italian wine and spirits exhibition. Like my fellow attendees, I had been tasting four or six hundred wines a day. One afternoon, feeling just drained by the end of a long day, my friend Elia and I headed off for dinner in an old Veronese inn, the Locanda di Castelvecchio. We were served pasta e fagioli for our first course, followed by a capon consommé with stuffed ravioli, and then an array of meats in a pot-au-feu with an anchovy-onion sauce. To accompany this festive meal, we selected a Bertani 1967 Amarone, which proved to be simply exceptional. In general, this estate's wines are compact and massive when young, but they become refined with age. The 1967 offered a divine harmony: its concentration had been transformed into complexity, its density into roundness, all accented with notes of confit fruits, spices, truffle, and mushrooms. We were so excited that we ordered a second bottle, a 1968 this time—purely for purposes of self-education, of course. Happy to have connoisseurs at table, the restaurateur joined us, explaining that very few customers opted for such old wines and were able to comprehend what makes them special.

The Veronese terroir also produces a dry white under the Soave appellation from an important Italian varietal, Garganega, as well as a sweet version, Recioto di Soave. With their strong, straight backbones, both age well too. And both wines deserve to bear their name proudly: these are indeed suave wines. The Soaves are genuinely gastronomic wines too, fine matches for gnocchi quattro formaggi or lake fish in agrodolce. Risi e bisi, a Venetian classic composed of rice boiled in broth, with green peas and parmesan, also suits a Soave perfectly.

Near Venice, we find a tiny winegrowing area long threatened by rising sea levels, where the Dorona di Venezia varietal yields wines with a strong iodine note. However, Venice is known above all for the quantities of prosecco drunk there, either alone or in cocktails like the Bellini (with fresh peach juice and pulp), Rossini (with strawberry coulis), or prosecco spritz (with Aperol or Campari). How many people today know that these cocktails, as well as the Americano (a Campari-and-vermouth spritzer)—in fact, the very first cocktails ever enjoyed anywhere—were all invented in Venice, at Harry's bar, in the Hotel Cipriani? It was indeed from Venice that cocktail culture spread throughout Europe, Great Britain, and the U.S. Traditionally, Venetians accompany their cocktails with cicchetti, an infinite variety of amuse-bouches made from meats, charcuterie, cheeses, vegetables, and fish—variously raw or fried, and appropriately seasoned. My advice: When in Venice, find yourself a nice piano bar and savor a local cocktail and some cicchetti for a memorable moment with a touch of poetry and glamour.

Gondoliers take a break at the Rialto Bridge in Venice.

Daily life in Venice.

"Venice is not only a city of of fantasy and and freedom. It is also a city of joy and pleasure." — Peggy Guggenheim

Since the eleventh century, gondolas have been an integral part of the city of Venice, now welcoming visitors for a unique perspective on the city. *Opposite:* Closing of the wine demijohns, 1959.

"The best Soave can age and evolve beautifully over several years, so there's always something new and intriguing to discover each time you return to the wine."

— Ian D'Agata, winegrower, Pieropan

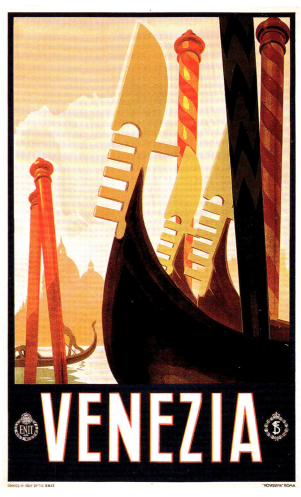

Northeastern Italy being a highly productive wine region, many unique wine shops can be found in Venice, providing visitors with one-of-a-kind varieties.

"Quality has been our passport to the world. It has allowed us to feel the pride of presenting a high-level Italian product." — Antonella and Emiliana Branca, Isolle Branca

Exploring—and tasting—the beauty of Venice ... and Venetian wine. *Following pages:* Fresh fish and homegrown cabbage will make for delicious homemade meals.

From the Venetian Lagoon to the Prosecco wine region, the Veneto offers an array of local wonders to explore. *Previous pages, from left:* Family moments shared around the table in the Veneto region; architectural wonders meet more modern details in a traditional Venetian villa. *Following pages, from left:* Taking the time to enjoy a summer wine tasting, in the surroundings of Venice; white grapes hang from wooden beams during a wine festival in Soave, Verona.

"When it comes to wine, the Veneto has much to be proud of."

— Enrico Bernardo

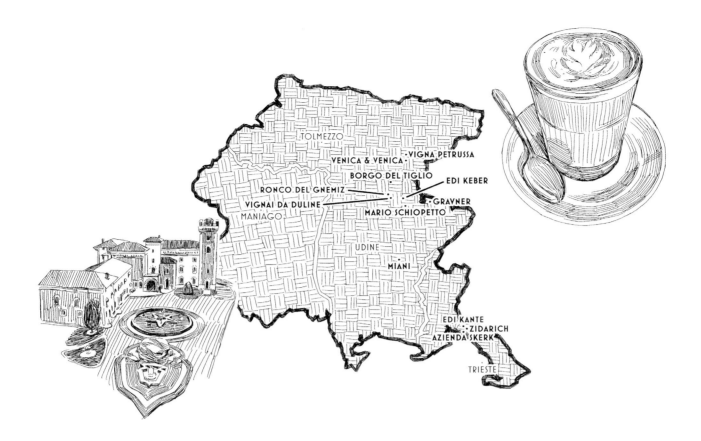

FRIULI

From Countryside to Literary Cafés

     Friuli extends north of Venice to Italy's borders with Slovenia to the east and Austria to the north. This frontier region has long had a unique and charming culture due to the intersection of Venetian and Austro-Hungarian influences. To stroll through Trieste's historic center, among the city's many literary cafés, is to enjoy a moment of pleasure suspended in time—the very same pleasure I feel when I taste Friulian wine.

     Friuli has enjoyed a fine reputation for the quality and variety of its wines, especially the whites, which encompass Ribolla, Friulano, Vitovska, Malvasia Istriana, Sauvignon, and Chardonnay. The last two—today considered "international varietals"—have since the nineteenth century been grown in Friuli, where their expression is dry, pure, and crystalline. As for the ancestral indigenous white cépages, we sometimes find them vinified through long maceration, using a very ancient technique originating in Armenia and Georgia, according to which the must is left on the skins for several days, weeks, or even months, often in amphorae or old casks. The wines take on an orangey hue and develop great intensity, becoming rich and aromatic while preserving their acidity. The winemaker using this method walks a tightrope: the result can be a thrilling masterpiece—or a cuvée with serious defects. Friulians have been making "orange wine" long before the recent vogue for it that has sprung up elsewhere. The original reason for adopting the method is a persistent need here to round off wines that are sometimes austere because the grapes fail to reach peak ripeness

Selecting the best wine to accompany some of
Italy's best local products and dishes.

by harvest time, yielding overly acidic juice lacking in aromatics. Friulian winemakers today have gained a following among their peers in other countries for their skill in this long-maceration technique, also now called "skin contact."

One real gem of this genre is found at the Skerk estate north of Trieste. The red earth here is so stony that the estate's workers must break through the crust and grind it into sand in order to plant each grapevine and enable it to put down roots. The wines aged in Skerk's amazing underground cellars present a strong, precise profile of great aromatic complexity and power, with exotic notes of apricot, orange, spices, honey, and bergamot. These wines are truly unusual: very dry on the tongue, with a long, persistent finish—lovely with cheeses. Skerk's Ograde cuvée in particular is unequaled in this style: unpretentious, dry yet appealingly mellow, with a highly evolved aroma but not oxidative. Ograde is impossible to categorize, content to be only itself: in a word, unique. Not just that, but it will not fade on you: leave a bottle open for two or three days and it just gets better.

Among producers of indigenous Friulian grapes, Edi Keber stands out. His estate is so close to the Slovenian border that one of his vineyards lies on the other side. Keber follows a strictly traditional method: a field blend and co-fermentation of the three top local cépages, Ribolla (the most acidic), Friulano (the fruitiest), and Malvasia (the most vegetal). The three grapes tend to ripen at different times, so Keber harvests over the course of two to three weeks, according to his vineyards' exposure. The result is a very lively, vibrant wine, naturally balanced, reasonably priced, and simply divine.

A third Friulian estate, by contrast, Edi Kante's, epitomizes just one grape, the local Malvasia. Kante's La Bora, named after the east wind, which adds to the influential ocean breezes, is saline, refined, subtle, and pure— magnificent with spaghetti alle vongole (with clams).

Among the Friulian estates that rely on international varietals, three deserve special mention. First, Miani's wines are highly structured and well balanced. Next, Ronco del Gnemiz makes Sauvignons and Chardonnays that, while inspired by their respective homeland terroirs in the Loire and Burgundy, are well adapted to local conditions. And finally, Vignai da Duline's Friuli Colli Orientali Pinot Grigio "Ronco Pitotti" is just delicious. It is worth noting that Friuli is a green and rainy region, like the Loire Valley, but with clay-limestone soils like Burgundy's and a continental climate like in Alsace—so it's no wonder all these French grapes are at home here.

Local Friulian reds are interesting too, with the indigenous varietals Schioppettino, Terrano, and Refosco dal Peduncolo Rosso at the forefront. All yield wines with a spicy, peppery nose and a lively but refined palate and are a good match for the local country fare: pork, game, polenta, cheeses, cabbage—and be sure to try a frico friulano, a crisp pancake made with potatoes, onions, and Montasio cheese, a hearty dish that recalls mountain cuisine. Yet all these Friulian reds are also good with lighter local specialties, such as the delicious San Daniele prosciutto.

To round off your visit to this lovely region, and your meal, there are two Friulian sweet dessert wines to try, both famous and highly prized: Picolit (made from the grape of the same name) and Ramandolo (made from Verduzzo). Both are late-harvest wines, sometimes botrytised: exuberant, open, exotic on the nose, and very subtle on the tongue.

The Livio Felluga vineyards punctuated by an array of trees.

161

"There are aromas, flavors, moments, that restore the natural rhythm of the seasons, that reconcile us with the world and with nature."

— *Livio Felluga, winegrower*

Winegrowing, a passion passed down from generation to generation in Friuli.

Peak of harvesting season in Friuli. *Following pages, from left:* Over the years, winemaker Livio Felluga has established his eponymous estate as one of the most beautiful and significant in Italy; art meets nature, making for the most memorable visit in the Friuli region.

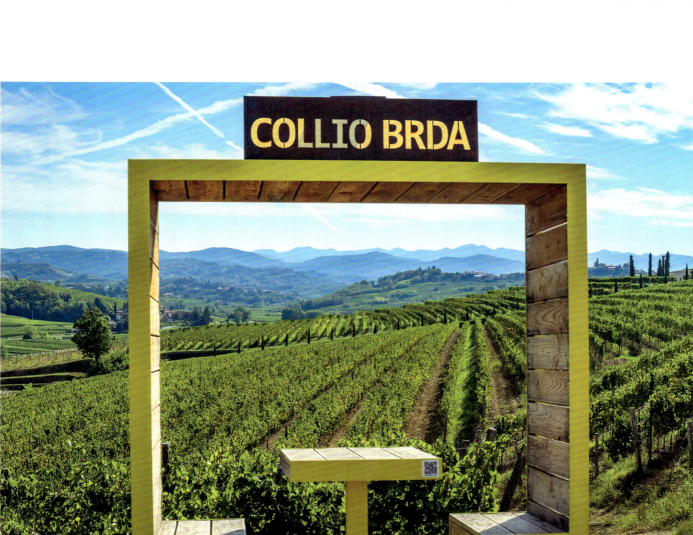

"Martissima is meant to be a provocation."

— Marta Venica, winegrower, Martissima Winery

In the heart of the Friuli region, wines are developed in the most natural way. *Following pages:* The lush vineyards of the Friuli region, where Colli Orientali wine is produced.

"I want to make wine.
I want to make
wine that is good, and then
there will be a consumer
who agrees with us."

—Josko Gravner, winegrower, Gravner

Local architecture and design treasures in Trieste.

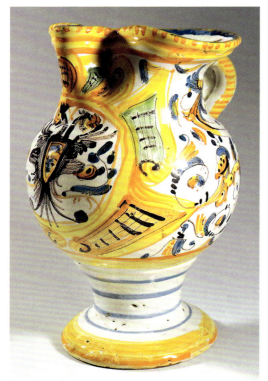

"By reducing yields and quantities, our grapes have always been able to give us full, true, healthy wines, the perfect expression of the land that hosts us and gives us life."

— Giuseppina, Hilde and Francesca Petrussa, winegrowers, Vigna Petrussa

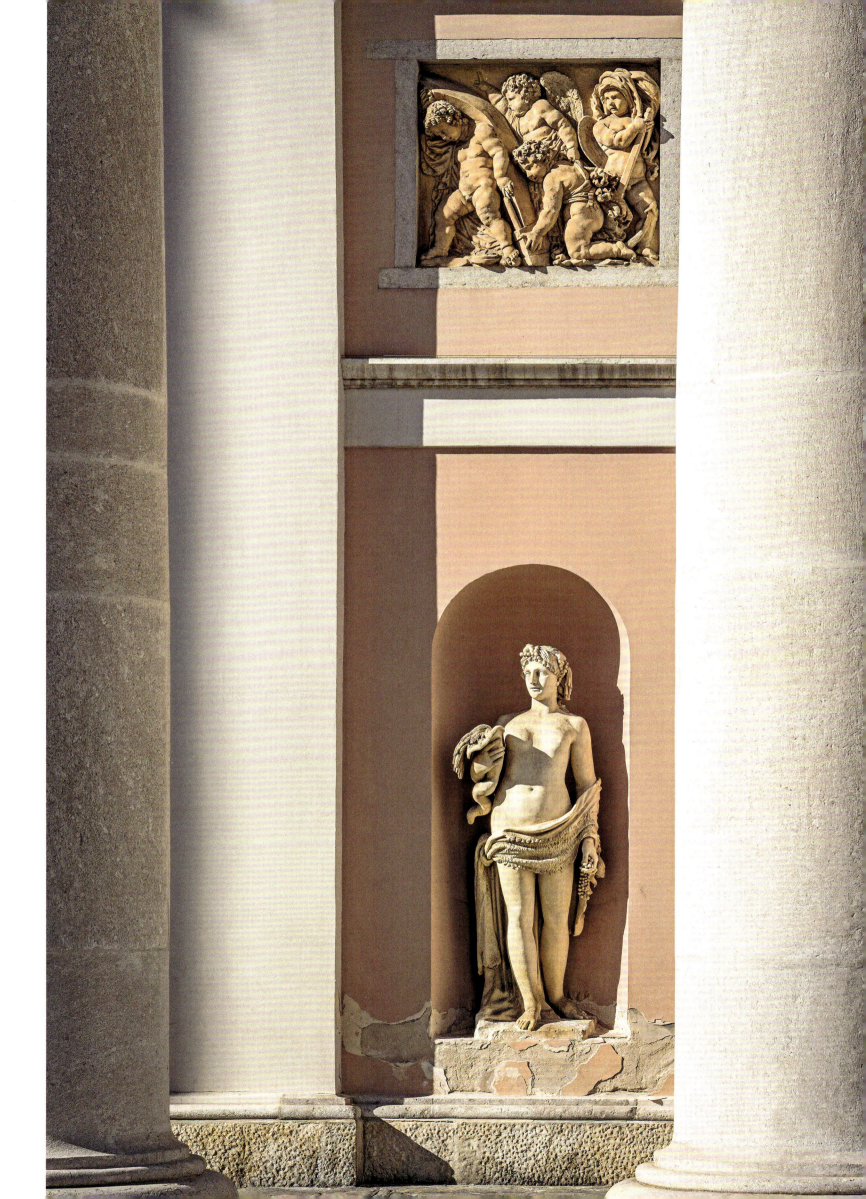

"*I wanted our wines to represent the vineyard, the land and our winemaking philosophy rather than rely on the success of a big-name-area.*"

— *Silvio Jermann, winegrower, Jermann Estate*

"To stroll through Trieste's historic
center, among the city's many
literary cafés, is to enjoy a moment
of pleasure suspended in time—
the very same pleasure I feel
when I taste Friulian wine."

— Enrico Bernardo

Spaghetti alle Vongole, fresh fish, and wine from the region around Trieste and Grignano. *Following pages, from left:* A bottle of Livio Felluga Abbazia di Rosazzo; homemade savory treats at Azienda Agricola Panegai.

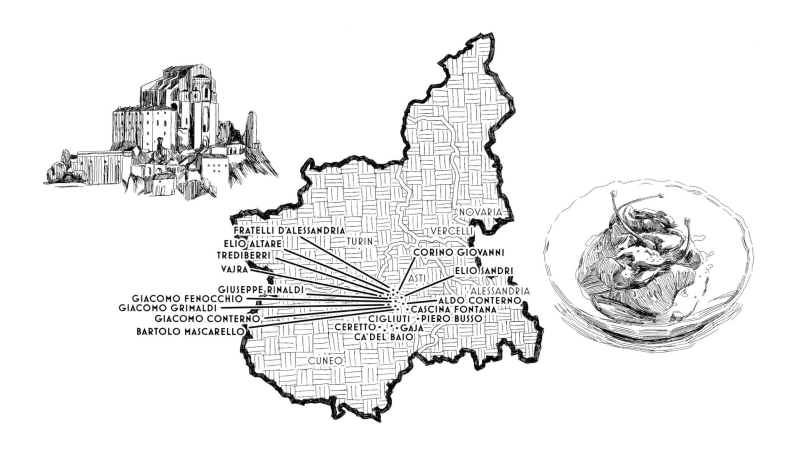

PIEDMONT

White Truffles, Hazelnuts, Barolo, and Barbaresco

If Piedmont is famed for a single gastronomical curiosity, it is this: from October to December every year, food and wine aficionados gather here for white-truffle season. It's a great time to hike. Diners can enjoy the delicacy in many typically Piedmontese ways: accenting a tartare or a piece of veal; on tajarin (a local fresh pasta similar to tagliarini); in scrambled eggs; in cheese fondue; and even on a hazelnut dessert. Such authentic Piedmontese dishes are rarely found outside the region. Truffle lovers receive a truly warm welcome too: even the smallest inn lavishes care and attention on feeding and housing visitors.

Truffle season aside, Piedmont is a region less well known to tourists than many others in Italy. Not only is it one of the few with no seacoast, but the Alps, looming only 80 kilometers/50 miles away, send their cold winds pouring down Piedmont's valleys—a boon for viticulture, but a turnoff for tourists, for whom Italy is often synonymous with summer heat. Piedmontese cuisine, of course, reflects the regional terroirs' character. The local Fassona breed of cattle yields the lean beef and veal featured in many dishes, including vitello tonnato, veal cooked in a court bouillon, sliced, and served cold in a mayonnaise-like sauce with tuna and often capers as well. Other specialties include oven-baked sausage-meat-stuffed onions in béchamel sauce and bagna cauda (raw vegetables dipped in a hot olive-oil-garlic-and-anchovy sauce, fondue style)—both examples of the region's typically rich fare.

Looking at the mountains surrounding Lake Maggiore. *Following pages:* The vineyards of the Giacomo Conterno, a historic estate producing one of Italy's most iconic wines, the Barolo Monfortino.

Piedmont's climate is marked by autumn mists. The top red varietal, Nebbiolo, a late-harvest grape, likes the cool nights at the end of the growing season. Indeed, the grape's name comes from nebbia, "fog," because, in the past, winegrowers would wait for the arrival of the autumn fogs before picking. The local landscapes by no means lack grandeur, boasting vineyard-contoured hillsides topped by ancient villages, with old red-tiled roofs, a church spire rising in the center, and a tower never far off. Indeed, the Langhe winegrowing district, famed for such lovely vistas, takes its name from the plural of an old dialect term, langa, meaning "elongated hill."

Of Piedmont's 41 DOCs and 19 DOCGs, two stand out Barolo, comprising eleven picture-postcard villages, and Barbaresco, four more. Here, and throughout the region, winegrowers maintain the ancestral practice of planting varietals according to altitude, because while the sloping vineyards offer every possible aspect, soils vary by elevation. Barbera, which is a touch acidic, and Nebbiolo, quite tannic, are planted high for maximum sun exposure. In the mid-levels we find early-ripening cépages such as the very fruity Dolcetto. Lower down, on heavier, damper soils, Muscat (Moscato Bianco) finds its ideal terroir; in the Asti DOCG, the grape is made into a sweet sparkler. Asti owes its success to its low alcohol level—7 to 9.5%; wines of the very similar Moscato d'Asti DOCG are lower still, at only 5.5% ABV—and its highly perfumed bouquet evoking fresh grapes. These Muscats are best with dessert—cakes and fruit. Walnut trees also flourish on the northern slopes of Piedmonts hill country, and are important to the regional economy.

For me, Piedmont somewhat recalls Burgundy: most of the estates remain family owned, most vineyard parcels are small, and many winegrowers share a commitment to making single-vineyard, even single-parcel wines without assemblage. In Barolo and Barbaresco, there are two schools of winemaking. The first, rooted in tradition, highlights complexity of bouquet and has always aged in big, old Slovenian oak foudres, relying on them for slow oxygenation, never for aromatic influence. Upon release,

Wine tasting at Anna Maria Abbona.

Unique experiences sampling local wine in Piedmont.

"We must take into account the past, but always project to the future."

— *Maria Germano, winegrower, Cantine Ettore Germano*

wines made from Nebbiolo in this way reveal earthy aromas and flavors of gentian, licorice, and plum—all maximally legible, without any cosmetic influence from oak. I particularly remember a 1959 Barolo from Borgogno and a 1985 Gaja Barbaresco, both wines that reflected their terroir, refined expressions of great character and complexity, smooth and with a long finish. Both were drinking at their peak, with notes of earth, white truffle, and bay leaf; wines of real distinction, without a trace of heaviness, but rather divinely light, beautiful—luminous, even sunny—and full, silky, yet built on a rugged frame. The second, newer, school relies on élevage in new barriques. The advocates of this approach (nicknamed, with a touch of irony, "the Barolo boys") decided in the late 1980s that they wanted to appeal to American consumers—the U.S. is by far the world's biggest importer of wine from Italy, in terms of both volume and sales—with darker, more structured, rounder, and frankly oakier wines. Accordingly, they opted to age in French barriques to give their wines a lightly toasted character, with fatter, more sugary tannins that blunt Nebbiolo's bitter edge. The two approaches have engendered lively debate ever since, with the traditionalists visibly shocked by what they consider the Barolo boys' iconoclasm, while the latter have nonetheless achieved ever-growing market success. Certain animosities aside, the proof is in the drinking. Today, Barolos and Barbarescos in both styles—wines from a traditionalist like Bartolo Mascarello and a modernist like Elio Altare, say—can be found side by side on the same wine list, and wine lovers can take their pick. And in the end, all of Piedmont's winegrowers have come out ahead.

Beyond the glories of Piedmont's two most glorious appellations are many others that deserve attention. Lying between Liguria and Lombardy, the Colli Tortonesi DOC offers white wines made from two local varietals, Timorasso and Favorita. Stony and sapid, these wines—cuvées from the Vigne Marina Coppi and Vigneti Massa estates, for example—are enormously appealing. So too are Benito Favaro's cuvées, from the Erbaluce de Caluso DOCG in northern Piedmont, with their attractive floral character and length. Other whites that share Erbaluce's saline note include wines from the Gavi, Roero (made from Arneis), and Alta Langa DOCGs, all delicious, for example, with fresh chèvre. The region's more affordable reds include Dolcetto from the Dogliani DOCG, with their purplish robe and fruity nose; the deep-purple wines of the Barbera d'Asti DOCG, with their wild-blackberry bouquet and lively palate; and Nebbiolos from Roero, pale garnet in hue, structured, and mouthwatering. These area all fine everyday wines, lip-smacking and well balanced, offering strong personalities and good value.

One of the larger winegrowing regions in Italy, Piedmont leads the way today because of its producers' success in improving both their wines' quality and their marketing. The region owes is renown in part to courageous winegrowers who stayed on their land at a time when the siren song of employers such as Fiat's factory in Turin and Ferrero's in Alba were emptying the countryside elsewhere in Italy. Among the many I could name, I would like to salute Angelo Gaja, Bruno Giacosa, the Ceretto family, and Renato Cigliuti in Barbaresco, and the Conterno, Mascarello, and Corino families in Barolo, all vineyard owners who believed in their destiny, and thereby saved viticulture in Piedmont.

Flying over the vineyards of the Barolo wine region during the fall season.

Piedmont provides a unique sensorial experience to visitors.

"The local landscapes by no means lack grandeur, boasting vineyard-contoured hillsides topped by ancient villages, with old red-tile roofs, a church spire rising in the center, and a tower never far off."

— Enrico Bernardo

"Piedmont is a haven for white truffle, which is closely linked to the gastronomy of the region, just like the wine is."

— Angélique de Lencquesaing, Idealwine

Curating moments to cherish in the Cuneo Province.
Following pages: Lush hills contrast against snowy mountains in Langhe.

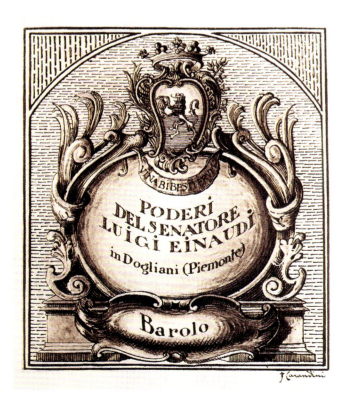

"Everyone likes elegance.
I believe that Barbaresco has the
opportunity of showing its beauty."

— Angelo Gaja, winegrower

Days spent foraging in nature and taking in the beauty of the Piedmont region.

THE SOUTH

———◆———

Molise, Basilicata, Puglia, and Calabria

I feel a particular attachment to southern Italy because its viticulture is all too often ignored—even forgotten. And yet what beautiful wines are made here!

Molise is renowned for the high quality of its durum wheat (used to make pasta), while Basilicata is renowned for its orchards. The four great rivers crisscrossing the south compensate for the hot meridional climate and partly account for its green landscapes and agricultural abundance. The list of notable products produced here comprises fruits (peaches, apricots, strawberries, figs), a variety of vegetables (eggplant, zucchini, tomatoes, peppers), the chicories (endive, escarole, radicchio), and many legumes—chickpeas, broad beans (favas), green peas. The south's interior highlands are heavily forested and yield mushrooms (including porcini, aka cep) and truffles. Hence the numerous dishes rooted in strong country cooking traditions, ranging from the simplest to the most complex: fried sweet peppers and Basilicata's Moliterno cheese; lightly spiced salumi flavored with aniseed (lovely with an aperitif); both handmade and die-cut pastas, including orecchiette, fusilli, and strascinati, sometimes served with a sausage-meat-and-tomato ragù.

To accompany all these beautiful southern flavors, there is one truly great red wine here, in the Aglianico del Vulture DOC, made from Aglianico grapes grown at the foot of the extinct Monte Vulture, harvested very late, and

At Paternoster, the vineyards are organic and rise to altitudes of 643 meters, their grapes yielding the most extraordinary volcanic wines.
Following pages: Lunch break during harvesting season in San Giorgio Lucano.

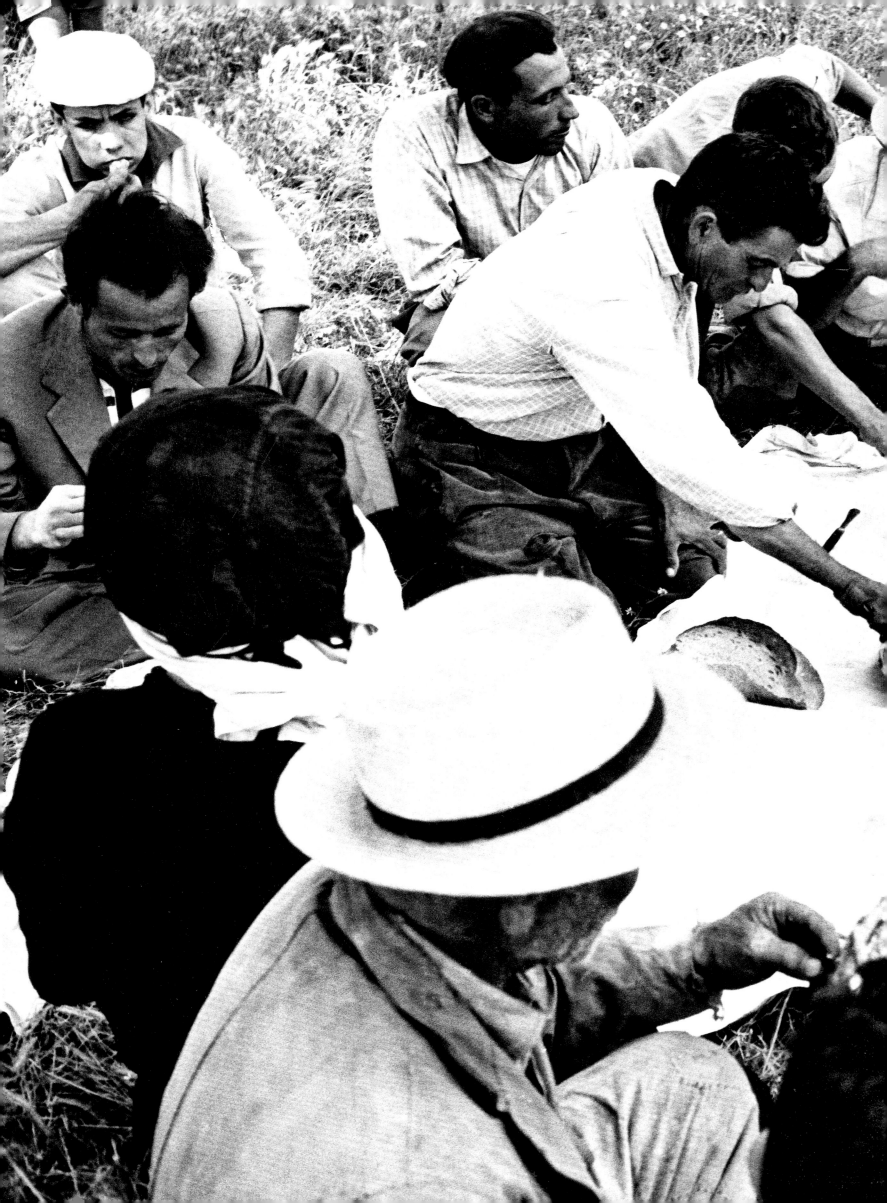

considered by wine lovers to be the "Barolo of the south." This is a tannic, highly structured wine that demands long aging. I happily recall enjoying with my family in Matera one of Elena Fucci's Aglianicos, a dense, full-bodied, succulent wine that had it all: a deeply rooted sense of its terroir, notes of eucalyptus, mint, and licorice. We enjoyed our bottle with Basilicata's famous strascinati in a tomato-meat sauce with sausage—delicious! This wine has recently begun to be better known and appreciated on the international market thanks in part to tourists' discovery of Matera, a lovely town, nicknamed the "second Bethlehem" because of the surprisingly biblical feel of its curious medieval architecture and layout, as well as its archeological importance (the site was first occupied by Paleolithic cave-dwellers).

Puglia is one of Italy's most heavily touristed regions, on account of the Baroque treasures of its cities and its fine beaches, mostly clustered around the heel of the Italian boot, and nicknamed the "Maldives of Italy" for their white sand and bright-blue water. Drier than Basilicata, Puglia produces excellent olive oils. Puglian cuisine is based on pastas and vegetables, as in the classic dish of pasta (especially orecchiete) with curly endive (cicoria), broccoli, or broccoli rabe and a touch of garlic or chili. Simpler but no less delicious is a slice from a big loaf of Altamura's distinctive sourdough bread, simply grilled, with a drizzle of olive oil.

In northern Puglia we find such varietals as Montepulciano (also grown in Molise), which here produces rather rich, fruity wines, many only drunk locally. Central Puglia's vineyards are better known, for their rich, tannic reds made from Negro Amaro or the quite perfumed and rounded reds of the Primitivo di Manduria DOC, which are much appreciated abroad. Puglian Primitivo (a sibling varietal of California's Zinfandel), and Manduria's in particular, offers pleasing notes of violet, licorice, and blackberry, seductively broad on the palate and quaffable. Primitivo's recent market success has helped to inaugurate a welcome period of advance in Puglian agriculture.

Calabria, forming the instep and toe of the Italian boot, with the Ionian Sea to the east and the Tyrrhenian Sea to the west, the fourth southern Italian wine region I highlight here, is a mystery to me—the most neglected southern terroir of all. But why? It is true that Calabria is hard to access by road—a four- to eight-hour drive from Naples, for example, depending on exactly where you want to go. The terrain here is mountainous and wild, with no really flat land. Calabrian cuisine and wine share the enticing boldness of the region's landscapes and the rooted authenticity of its people.

Calabria was one of the first parts of Italy settled by Greek colonists (in the eighth century BCE), and one of the first places where they planted Greek vines—with, ultimately, great success. Today, the wines grown in the part of Calabria closest to Sicily (where the Greeks first settled in the region, in fact) are quite elegant, but with a freshness that distinguishes them from Calabrian wines grown farther north. Of the latter, the Cirò DOC has long been outstanding.

It will perhaps be obvious that there is a lot for wine lovers to discover in Calabria, which also offers the great advantage of astonishingly good wines at low prices. The Greco di Bianco DOC, for example, a copper-colored passito dessert wine, boasts mineral notes, with a surprising burst of unusual wild-herb and spice flavors. Calabria is also recognized for its proud culinary traditions. Bergamot and licorice feature in pastry and cosmetics, and the region boasts an impressive variety of fish and seafood, including anchovies, oily fish (tuna, sardines, mackerel), all best enjoyed with the refreshing, saline-accented local white wines.

Scenes in and around Matera. *Following pages, from left:* The magnificence of Matera has inspired many artists over the decades, including Carlo Levi and Giovanni Pascoli; summer nights in Calabria.

"The factors that make a perfect glass of Italian wine? Balance, elegance, varietal character, sense of place, versatility with food, and impeccable value for the price."

— Leonardo LoCascio, Winebow Imports

Calabria's wine production is more than ninety percent reds, and has been subject to many influences in the past centuries. *Following pages, from left:* At Cantine Del Notaio, the passion for winemaking has been handed down for seven generations; organic-wine-and-olive-oil producer Roberto Ceraudo.

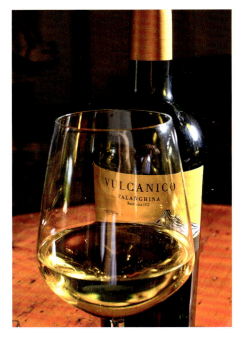

Local flavors and activities by the sea in the heart of Calabria.
Previous pages: Inside the Chiesa del Purgatorio, in Matera.
Following pages, from left: Traditional dress of the region; Calabrian produce, grown on local grounds.

RISTORANTE
PIZZERIA

VECCHIO
GRANAIO

FORNO
A LEGNA

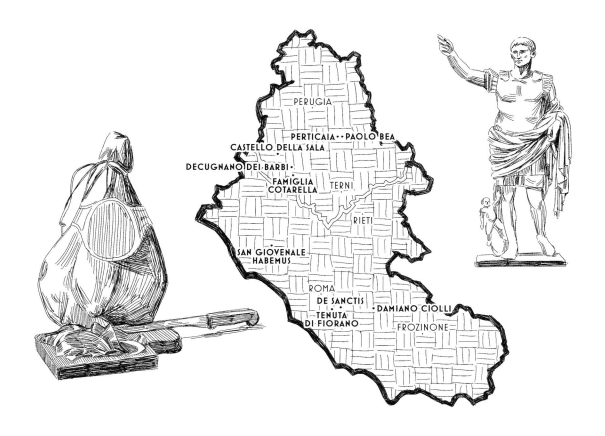

LAZIO AND UMBRIA

From Rome to Assisi

Rome and Lazio, the region surrounding the ancient city, constitute the finest open-air museum of all time. Built at the very heart of the Mediterranean basin, the Eternal City offers layer upon layer of history, not only of the Roman Republic and Empire but of Etruscan, Greek, Barbarian, Arab, and Byzantine civilizations—and, for the last two thousand years, the Catholic Church. From the earliest basilicas through the glories of the Baroque to nineteenth-century revival styles, the entire history of Christian architecture is on display here, with some churches just a few steps from ancient monuments like the Colosseum and the Forum. At the heart of Rome stands Vatican City, surrounding St. Peter's Basilica, which was built atop the tomb of the first pope, and the Vatican Museums, which house one of the greatest concentrations of artistic masterpieces on Earth.

Yet Rome is also the realm of la dolce vita, familiar worldwide from countless moments in film that celebrate love and the good life: tourists throwing coins in the Trevi Fountain to ensure their return; narrow, winding streets where little Fiats compete with Vespas; intimate tree-shaded squares. And, of course, food and wine. I recall, for example, a meal of pasta alla carbonara with a Cesanese del Piglio red. What could be simpler and more seductive than this marriage of flavors, which no refinement could possibly improve?

Lazio (ancient Latium), shares the city's spirit: its people are sociable, cheerful, extroverted; they love a good time with friends. The region's cuisine is as varied as any other in Italy, with an emphasis on home cooking—Italian

comfort food. Everything revolves around dry pasta in multiple forms napped in sauces of all kinds: alla carbonara, cacio e pepe, all' amatriciana, alla gricia, alla puttanesca . . . Yet there are many other equally classic dishes not to be missed: abbacchio, suckling lamb, prepared in several ways; carciofi alla giudia, deep-fried artichokes; braised chicory; gnocchi alla romana, oven-baked semolina gnocchi; bean soup; saltimbocca alla romana, pan-fried veal wrapped in prosciutto and sage leaves; bruschetta; deep-fried zucchini blossoms . . . To accompany these dishes, Lazio produces wines that are fruity, round, lively, and often good when young, wines whose freshness balances the flavors of tomato and onion, the richness of a carbonara, or the density of variety meats, which are often featured here. Many of these wines have been made for centuries and share a sunny, even a joyful character. Outstanding examples include wines from the Frascati, Castelli Romani, and Est! Est!! Est!!! di Montefiascone DOCs. According to a (likely apocryphal) tradition, the wines of Montefiascone—made from Trebbiano and Malvasia, floral, fruity, and refreshing—have been favored by popes and prelates for centuries. Farther inland, the Cesanese del Piglio DOCG offers full, rounded reds: light-colored, with a delicately aromatic nose, an attractive fruitiness, and delectable notes of rose and raspberry—a happy match with sauced pasta dishes or a pizza shared in Rome's Trastevere neighborhood.

About three hours by train or car from Rome in the region of Umbria, immediately north of Lazio, Assisi makes for a fine excursion for visitors interested in Church history—and wine. Umbria is one of the handful of Italian regions with no seacoast, although it does have one big lake, Trasimeno, and a smaller one, Corbara, which help to create a gentle microclimate for the dry white wines of the Orvieto DOC, which overlaps Lazio and Umbria. There are also a few exceptional botrytised dessert wines made from grapes grown on the hillsides in the Lago di Corbara DOC, where the morning fogs and Indian summer heat are perfect for this style.

Beyond its ancient towns and villages with an international reputation, such as Gubbio, Spello, Todi, Norcia, Perugia, and Assisi (a global pilgrimage site), Umbria is somewhat more rural in character than Tuscany or Lazio, and less touristed, which has enabled Umbrians to preserve their authentic way of life. Umbria produces significant quantities of wheat and olives; the latter are used to accent charcuterie and sauced dishes, in the spirit of simple country cooking. Wine lovers will enjoy pairing local specialties like scrambled eggs with wild asparagus with Orvieto whites made from Grechetto. Among local reds, those from the Montefalco Sagrantino DOCG and Torgiano DOC are both intriguingly structured wines that go well with local antipasti, such as prosciutto from Norcia—or even better with a fillet of young wild boar or umbrichelli (a thick, chewy Umbrian spaghetti) with black truffles, which are abundant locally. In Umbria, you can eat and drink like a king (or a pope)—even on a budget.

Umbria's rural landscapes are enthralling, sensual, with some hillsides gently sloping, others steep. The land here was once an ancient seabed, and it is rich in sand, limestone, clay, and tufa; in Orvieto, the marine sedimentary layers even include shells and other fossils. Umbria's environment is also very healthy, with its abundance of lakes and forests and an emphasis on polyculture. Many Umbrian winegrowers are quite naturally drawn to organic and biodynamic techniques.

I recall one Orvieto white, about twenty years old, with a strong iodine note on the nose—superb. Many wine lovers have only a hazy idea of what a mature Italian white wine can be. They are out there to be found, though, bringing us notes of stone and smoke from the soil and subsoils in which they grow. Just give them time to age in bottle, and they reveal their true excellence.

Enclaved within Rome, Vatican City is a bastion of iconic art and architecture. *Following pages, from left:* A unique piece with the effigy of Benedict XVI Papacy can be seen in the Chinese Room of the Apostolic Palace, the summer residence of the popes in Castel Gandolfo, near Rome; known for its notable green highlights, Cervaro della Sala has an intense, complex nose.

"Palazzone wines represent the vocation of the place, transferring in their quality the uniqueness of the soil, tradition and artisan culture."

— Pietro Dubini, winegrower, Palazzone

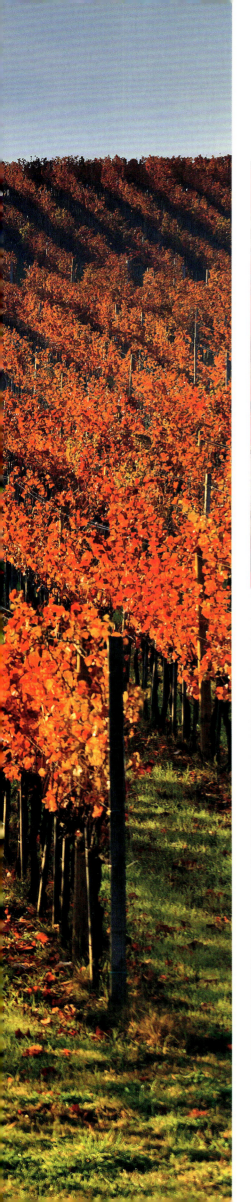

Visiting the Vatican, or the world's smallest state. *Opposite:* The vibrant colors of a local Umbrian vineyard.

"Rome, and Lazio, the region surrounding the ancient city, constitute the finest open-air museum of all time."

— Enrico Bernardo

Spending time with friends and family, harvesting grapes and tasting wine in the region. *Following pages:* Excellent wine and cuisine make for the perfect evening at Enoteca del Frate, in Rome.

"Today, in addition to the essential quality of the grapes, creating excellent wines requires vision, innovation and nerve."

— Leonardo and Luca Baccarelli, winegrowers, Cantina Roccafiore

Rome enchants locals and foreigners alike with its exquisite food and friendly atmosphere. *Following pages:* Rome seen from St. Peter's Basilica.

"Our philosophy is inspired by its terroir—the idea that wines must be the individual expression of their soil, climate and cultivation in the vineyard."

— *Fusco family,*
Merumalia Wine Resort

Magical light and moments in Rome, or la dolce vita. *Following pages, from left:* The unmatched beauty of St. Peter's Basilica, in Vatican City; Gian Lorenzo Bernini, *Angel with Scroll,* inside the Sant Andrea delle Fratte church, in Rome.

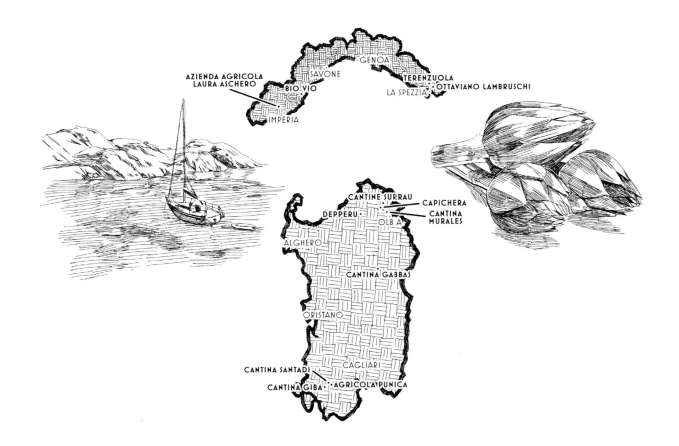

LIGURIA AND SARDINIA

Between Land and Sea, from Portofino to the Costa Smeralda

It is neither by chance nor in memory of the ancient House of Savoy (which ruled Sardinia from 1720 to 1861) that I have chosen to treat these two winegrowing regions together, separated though they are by an expanse of ocean. Both the Ligurian coast and the island of Sardinia are home to vineyards typical of those on Mediterranean shores as well as others just a few hundred paces inland—typically terraced in Liguria, and in Sardinia surrounded by meadowland. In Liguria, the maritime influence may mingle in the region's wines with forest floor and mushroom notes; on the island, it is complemented by aromas of the maquis scrubland, like myrtle and wild herbs.

The two terroirs also share a dominant white varietal, Vermentino, one of the pillars of Mediterranean winegrowing, which also excels in Provence, Corsica, and on the Tuscan coast. I consider Vermentino the Riesling of the south, sharing that grape's lively minerality, its notes of clementine and sage. Wines made from Vermentino are pleasing, floral, yet dry; their caressing, glyceric mouth feel is a pleasure in itself, and they age well too, taking on smoky notes—all advantageous for the flavors of Mediterranean cuisine. Indeed, Liguria and Sardinia also share a very specific style of cuisine that I like to think of as "between land and sea." Both regions offer delicious shellfish and crustaceans, but also flavorsome meats. Accordingly, outstanding examples of traditional Sardinian dishes include linguini with spiny (aka rock) lobster or bottarga, and suckling pig oven-roasted overnight with a few branches of

Savoring fresh shrimp on a boat in the port of Cinq Terre. *Following pages:* Overlooking Cinque Terre, in Liguria.

myrtle and rosemary. Similarly, Liguria boasts trofie or trofiette (a twisted short pasta) with pesto, as well as fillet of red mullet with raw purple artichokes, branzino with Taggiasca olives, squid stuffed with mushrooms and firm-textured trombetta summer squash (delicious puréed), and rabbit with Swiss chard. Throughout Liguria, it is common to be served heaping plates of anchovies, ravioli stuffed with goat cheese in walnut-and-pine-nut sauce, or cima alla genovese, a poached stuffed breast of veal. The two regions each boast unique specialties too, of course, such as their breads: focaccia alla genovese is enjoyed throughout Liguria, not only in the capital of Genoa, while Sardinia is famed for its crisp flatbread, pane carasau.

Ligurian wines are luminous in color, floral and perfumed on the nose, and light in structure. Not to be missed are Laura Aschero's floral Rossese, complementing barely seared red mullet with black olives and a branch of marjoram, say; and Claudio Vio's aromatic Pigato Riviera Ligure di Ponente, perhaps with the first green asparagus of spring seasoned with lemon, olive oil, and a few mint leaves; and the intense flavors of Terenzuola's Vermentino Colli di Luni, with trofie in pesto.

Because of its strategically important position, Sardinia was conquered serially by Carthage, the Vandals, Byzantium, Genoa, Pisa, Aragon, Spain, Savoy, and Piedmont. All left traces behind. In Alghero, a village in the north of the island, Catalan is spoken, while on Carloforte, an islet off the coast of Cagliari, in the south, you hear Genoese dialect. Several varietals of Spanish origin have long thrived in Sardinia, such as Carignano (aka Cariñena, Carignan), Cannonau (aka Garnatxa, Grenache), and Vernaccia di Oristano. This Vernaccia is vinified in an oxidative style, like sherry, and aged in chestnut casks in contact with air—that is, with no topping up of the barrels (ouillage) to prevent oxidation—which enables development of the precious flor that gives the wine its signature dried-fruit notes. Several other whites produced on the island have earned an appellation of their own, including the DOCs of Malvasia di Bosa and Moscato di Sorso-Sennori, and the Vermentino di Gallura DOCG. Gallura estates like Capichera, Cantina Depperu, and Vigne Surrau are always good bets. For a splendid summer meal, match any of their wines with a dish of pasta and spiny lobster: the marriage of iodine and mineral flavors on the plate and in the glass and the round, caressing finish of these wines is just perfection. Sardinia also produces very interesting reds in the Carignano del Sulcis and Cannonau DOCs. Gabbas's Cannonaus pair marvelously with roast suckling pig; Giba's Carignanos, with lamb chops.

Whether it's a Ligurian or a Sardinian wine you're after, both regions offer idyllic places to enjoy it. From the charming fishing village of Portofino on the Italian Riviera, to the historic villages of the Cinque Terre farther up the Ligurian coast, to Sardinia's chic Costa Smeralda, paradise is never far away.

The bright, typical architectural details of Sardinia. *Following pages:* Vernazza, Liguria, in 1959.

"Both the Ligurian coast and the island of Sardinia are home to vineyards typical of those on Mediterranean shores."

— Enrico Bernardo

Traditional celebrations and local products and grapes in the Sassari province.
Following pages, from left: Make sure to stop for some handmade pasta when visiting Sardinia; Sella & Mosca promises that "both eyes and palate will love this land."

"Decugnano dei Barbi is a silent witness to the passing of time, a guardian of vinous treasures, and a tribute to the soul that still permeates the air of Santa Maria di Decugnano."

— Claudio Barbi, winegrower, Decugnano dei Barbi

Sunny days spent on the hills of Sardinia over the decades.

Restful afternoons on the coast of Sardinia.

"The vines grow in clay and calcareous based soils, rich in fossil shells, and they are well exposed to the rising of the sun with an excellent difference of temperature between day and night." — Marchese Piero, winegrower, Marchesi Antinori

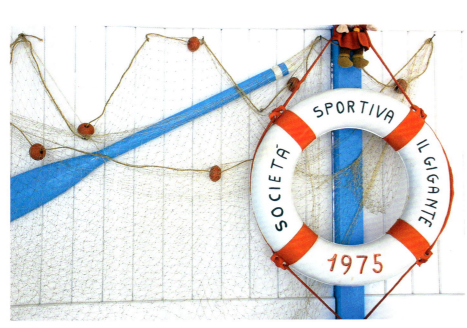

Getting ready for an afternoon on the water around the Mediterranean.
Following pages: Walking along the cliffs of Capo Caccia.

Reflecting on time spent in Cinque Terre. *Opposite:* Sailing around Cinque Terre.

"We strongly believe in our territory, in its wine culture and tradition and we intend to communicate all this to the world through a bottle capable of transmitting our values on its own."

— Alberto Mario Pardi, winegrower, Cantina Fratelli Pardi

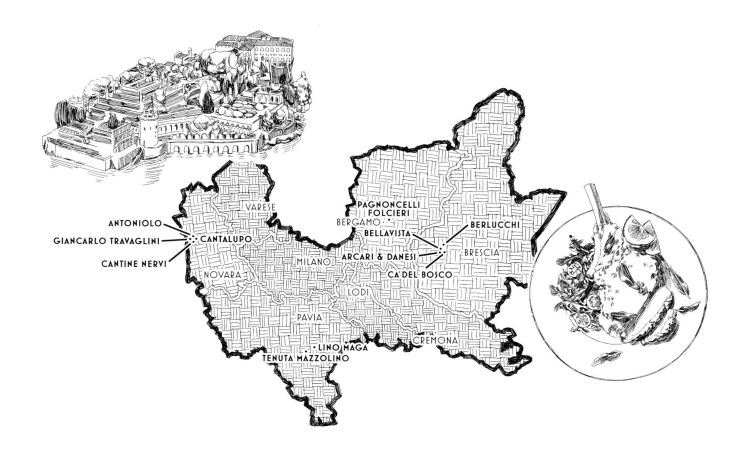

THE ITALIAN LAKES

Lake Maggiore, Lake Iseo, Lake Como, and Lake Garda

These four lakes are the largest of Lombardy's numerous lakes. All four offer magnificent views and elegant tourist destinations. And this realm of Riva yachts is yet another region of Italy where wine reigns in triumph. Here, north of the Po Plain, far from the Mediterranean, the rough winds that descend from the Italian Alps in the distance is moderated by the lake country's microclimate.

Centered around Milan, the regional capital, Lombardy's cuisine melds influences from the mountains, plains, and lakes, including such specialties as bresaola (air-dried, salt-cured beef), freshwater fish, and many kinds of risotto (with mushrooms, asparagus, artichokes, or green peas, or alla milanese—with saffron—to name just a few). Pork, veal, and poultry are equals here, and all are well matched by local wines. Enjoy cotoletta alla milanese (veal coated in breadcrumbs, fried in butter) with a San Colombano Barbera; cosce di rane all'aglio e prezzemolo (frogs' legs with garlic and parsley) with an Oltrepò Pavese spumante; lake trout in agrocolce with a fruity Lugana white; pumpkin-stuffed tortelli alla mantovani with a sparkling, refreshing Franciacorta.

Lake Maggiore, on the border of Lombardy and Piedmont, is enchantingly beautiful, lined with prestigious historic great hotels, especially in Stresa, with its old-world ambience of refined high-society glamour. While overlooking the lake, enjoy a glass of a red from the Ghemme or Gattinara DOCGs. Both are made, like Barolo, from Nebbiolo, and

Overlooking Lake Como from one of the luxurious rooms at Hotel Passalacqua. *Following pages, from left:* Breathtaking views of the neighboring properties at Villa d'Este, in Cernobbio; in 1961, winemaker Guido Berlucchi (pictured here) created the region's first classic-method wine—the Franciacorta—with Franco Ziliani.

"A glass of Berlucchi contains no compromises, only the highest quality."

— Guido Berlucchi

both benefit from the gentle microclimate of their hilly lakeside terroirs, which enable the grape skins to reach perfect ripeness. Both offer roundness, with a firm tannic tissue that makes an ideal match for tender, unctuously rich braised dishes like osso buco—or goes equally well with a cèpes risotto or polenta with a ragù of small game birds.

Around Lake Como and Lake Iseo, we come to the Valcalepio DOC and the Franciacorta DOCG. Here, between the plain and the lakes, Cabernet Sauvignon and Merlot are made into still wines, while Pinot Nero, Pinot Bianco, and Chardonnay are made into sparklers. Near Bergamo, we also find a very rare sweet wine made from a late-harvest red by the name of Moscato di Scanzo (the name of both the DOCG and the grape). It is delicious with gorgonzola on grilled country bread or with a coupe of wild strawberries.

The sloping vineyards on the Lombardy side of Lake Garda produce rather fresh, refreshing, aromatic wines: Lugana, a white made from Trebbiano, and the Riviera del Garda Classico red, made from Marzemino, Groppello, Barbera, and Sangiovese. On the Venetian side of the lake, near Verona, the reds and rosés of Bardolino are quite light and tasty, as are the whites of Custoza. All these wines are much appreciated by the hordes of tourists who descend on the region in summer, especially from Germany.

South of the lakes, in the heart of the Po Plain, the region of Oltrepò Pavese offers lightly sparkling reds made from Pinot Nero, Croatina, and Bonarda, which marry marvelously with the local charcuterie and with Milanese dishes like veal kidney or tongue and other variety meats—winter dishes high in fat, accompanied by rice or potatoes rather than pasta. This region is also home to a true gem, grown in a hillside vineyard considered a grand cru equivalent: Azienda Agricola Barbacarlo. Here, legendary winegrower Lino Maga, nicknamed "il signor Barbacarlo," made magnificent wines from century-old vines for decades prior to his death in 2022, using indigenous yeasts exclusively. Barbacarlo is rustic and highly variable from year to year, but a perfectly aged bottle from a good year is pure magic. I have been lucky several times to savor this nectar after a few years in the cellar—it's always a magnificent surprise (and easy on the stomach too).

Lombardy can be a foggy place, but the mists seem to lift whenever you sit down with friends to enjoy a glass of Franciacorta in one hand and some local delicacy in the other. Whether you are at table in Bergamo's historic center, lakeside, or in downtown Milan, there is simply no better aperitif.

Harvesting grapes at Bellavista winery in Franciacorta, in Lombardy.

Full of emblematic and one-of-a-kind vineyards, the Lake region is
one of the best for wine lovers to visit in the North of Italy.

"My philosophy of Italian wines is that wine was created to be consumed with food. Truly great wines all have their own individual character."

— *Franco Ziliani, Italian wine expert*

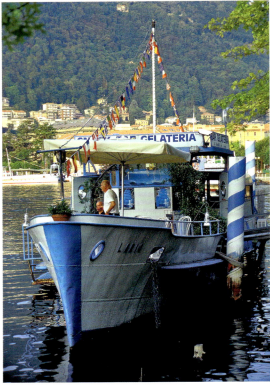

Quality time spent on the water in the Lake region. *Following pages, from left:* Originally called Villa del Garovo, Villa d'Este provides visitors with unparalleled views of Lake Como; Villa Carlotta's botanical garden is home to monumental trees, English roses, and citrus tunnels for guests to enjoy.

"In the mid-90s, the oenologists started stylizing wines. That was a revolution for Italian wine."

— James Suckling, wine critic

The luxury hotels and local vineyards offer visitors both fascinating visits and quality downtime.

"Our cellar is the beating heart of our winery.
It is where our wine rests, changes and evolves."

— Cinzia Travaglini, winegrower, Travaglini Gattinara

Summer days around Lake Como. *Following pages, from left:* On the tip of the promontory of Lavedo, Villa Balbianello overlooks Isola Comacina and the western shore of Lake Como; an example of the lush hills that surround lakes and vineyards in the region.

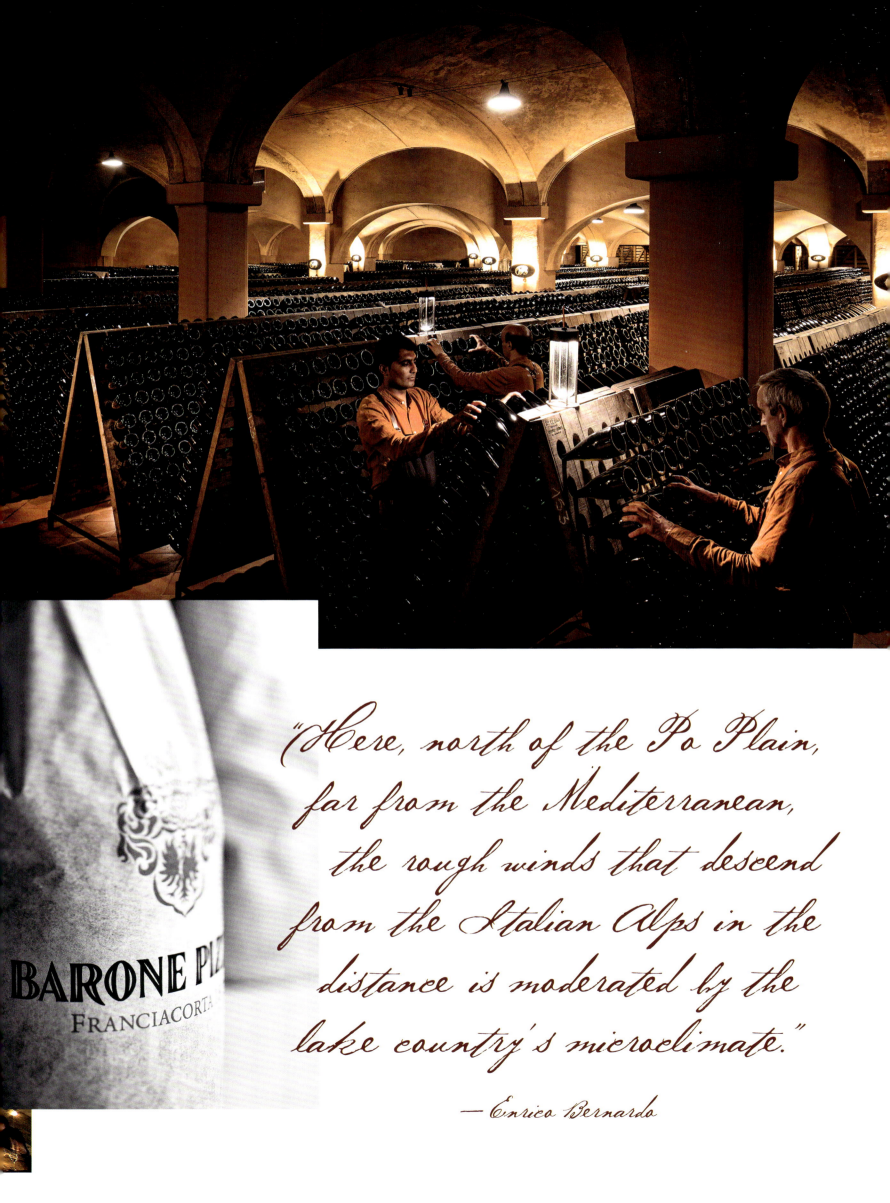

"Here, north of the Po Plain, far from the Mediterranean, the rough winds that descend from the Italian Alps in the distance is moderated by the lake country's microclimate."

— Enrico Bernardo

"From nature we learn the need to transform ourselves,
to renew the will and thoughts. From it we learn the
meaning of waiting, the gift of patience and the pleasure
of generosity. Nature itself is the greatest utopia.
It's the best of all possible worlds. It is the essence
of every non-there and of every not yet."

— Francesca Moretti, winegrower, Bellavista Franciacorta

Dinner by the shore after a day of exploring the Lake region. *Following pages:* In the heart of Lombardy, Lecco lies at the southern end of Lake Como.

GLOSSARY

APPASSIMENTO	The Italian equivalent of the French term passerillage: the process of partially drying grapes prior to pressing in order to concentrate their sugar, resulting in sweeter, more alcoholic wine. Traditionally, the grapes were dried on straw mats; today, metal trays of various kinds are much more common. Several famed Italian wines are made this way, including Amarone, Recioto, and Vin Santo.
ASSEMBLAGE	The blending of wine from different grape varietals, vineyards, vintages, or crus prior to bottling in order to create a specific bouquet and flavor profile; the term refers to both the blending process and the resulting blend. The Italian equivalent is assemblaggio.
AZIENDA AGRICOLA	"wine estate": A winegrowing farm that produces its own wine. This term occurs at the beginning of many winegrowing estates' official names, so much so that it is simply understood and often omitted. It is distinct from azienda vinicola, which designates a winemaking firm that buys most or all of its grapes from growers.
BARRIQUE	An oak barrel or cask for aging wine after vinification and élevage and prior to bottling. Capacity varies greatly; in France, about 200 liters/53 U.S. gallons is typical. French barriques are used for aging in some parts of Italy, most notably in Piedmont.
BIANCO	"white"
CANTINA	"cellar," winery: This term appears at the beginning of many Italian wine estate names, before the Azienda Agricola portion, if there is one.
CÉPAGE	Wine grape variety (aka varietal). Cépage is sometimes also used as the equivalent of encépagement, to refer to the varietals in a field or a cellar blend.
CRU	Vineyard producing wine grapes, especially one formally graded as to the quality of its annual production.
CUVÉE	"vatful": A specific wine. Depending on context, this word can in effect be synonymous with the terms vintage, assemblage/blend, or, for estates that release more than one wine, label.
DOLCE	"sweet"
DENOMINAZIONE	"denomination," equivalent to appellation: The modern Italian wine classification system was introduced in 1963, modeled on France's appellation d'origine contrôlée (AOC) laws. The system has since been adjusted multiple times to harmonize with evolving European Union regulations. Like the AOC classifications, Italy's are equivalent to those in the newer, EU-mandated appellation d'origine protégée ("protected designation of origin," AOP) system. As in France, Italian wine producers are permitted, and almost all prefer, to continue using their own nation's terminology on their labels.

The Italian system includes four main designations. At the base of the hierarchy is the denominazione di origine (designation of origin), or DO level, which is rarely encountered (and does not occur in this book); likewise, the term vino da tavola ("table wine," equivalent to the French vin de table) is seldom seen on wine labels and does not occur here. For the upper three levels of the Italian wine appellation/ denominazione system, see DOC, DOCG, and IGT below.

DENOMINAZIONE DI ORIGINE CONTROLLATA, DOC

"controlled designation of origin": The third level up in Italy's appellation system; DOC is also used informally to refer to the system as a whole. Wines labeled DOC are from regions subject to multiple rules and regulations governing permitted grape varieties, oak aging, and the boundaries of the geographic area defined as the DOC. Only about 30 percent of Italian wine is classified as DOC or the highest level of all, DOCG (see below).

DENOMINAZIONE DI ORIGINE CONTROLLATA E GARANTITA, DOCG

"controlled and guaranteed designation of origin": The fourth and highest level of Italy's appellation system, the peak of the pyramid. DOCG wines must meet all DOC qualifications and must be bottled in the same area of production and undergo a taste test by the local Ministry of Agriculture. In many DOCs, riserva wines constitute a DOCG with the same appellation name.

ÉLEVAGE

"raising, bringing up" (as in rearing children or livestock): A French term designating the progression of all the stages between fermentation and bottling, including aging (in vat, tank, barrel, amphora, etc.), fining, and filtering.

ENCÉPAGEMENT

The relative proportions of the different grape varieties grown in a single vineyard or on an entire estate, or of those used to make a particular blend. The term can also refer to grapes all of the same varietal but grown in different vineyards or in different vineyard parcels.

ESTATE

A winegrowing property, which may range from tiny to vast. Related Italian terms include: azienda agricola (see above); cascina, fattoria, or podere ("farmhouse" or "farm," a rural estate); and tenuta, all of which occur in the names of Italian winegrowing estates and on their products' labels.

FOUDRE

A French term for a large (sometimes colossal) cask used for maturing, storing, and even transporting wine. Foudres are significantly larger than typical oak barrels, often holding more than a thousand liters. In Barolo and Barbaresco, Slovenian oak foudres play an important role in the traditional style of vinification.

INDICAZIONE GEOGRAFICA TIPICA, IGT

"indication of geographical typicality": The second level in Italy's appellation system, above DO.

MACERATION

Process of soaking grape skins—and maybe pulp, seeds, and stems—in grape juice during winemaking.

MAQUIS	Dense, scrubby vegetation made up of evergreen shrubs and small trees, characteristic of many Mediterranean coastal areas. The word derives from the Corsican Italian dialect word macchia. An herbal maquis note is often present in the aroma of Sardinian wines.
MUST	The pulp and skins of the crushed grapes before and during fermentation
PASSITO	A wine made using the appassimento process (see above).
RISERVA	"reserve": A wine aged longer and usually of higher quality than the norm for its style; many DOCs include a DOCG appellation for their riserva releases.
ROSATO	rosé
ROSSO	red
SECCO	dry
SINGLE-VARIETAL	An unblended wine, one made from only a single grape variety. Still more restricted are single-vineyard and single-parcel cuvées.
SLOPE AND ASPECT	The steepness and the compass orientation (hence the sun exposure and prevailing winds) of hillside or mountainside vineyards—critical aspects of terroir (see below).
TERROIR	A given geographic area with specific environmental and human features that define an agricultural product's essential characteristics; terroir includes soil, topology, and climate; farming and processing practices; and other aspects of traditional savoir faire that contribute to the production of agricultural products of all kinds.
VIN SANTO	"Holy Wine": A traditional wine style of Tuscan dessert wine characterized by an exceptionally long, slow fermentation of sweet juice from dried grapes in sealed barrels.
VINTAGE	The year in which a wine is produced. The Italian equivalent is annata. With reference to sparkling wines, the term millesimato is also used.

ENRICO BERNARDO'S IDEAL WINE CELLAR

THE ALPS

VALLE D'AOSTA
ANSELMET
ERMES PAVESE
GROSJEAN
LES CRÊTES
OTTIN VINI

VALTELLINA
AR.PE.PE.
CASA VINICOLA ALDO RAINOLDI
DIRUPI
FAY SANDRO

THE DOLOMITES
ABRAHAM
ALOIS LAGEDER
BOLOGNANI
CANTINA COLTERENZIO
CANTINA MOSER TRENTO
CANTINA TERLANO
CASTEL JUVAL
CESCONI
FERRARI
FORADORI
GUMP HOF
HARTMANN DONÀ
IGNAZ NIEDRIST
KÖFERERHOF
LIESELEHOF
LUNELLI (FERRARI)
MANNI NÖSSING
MASO MARTIS
NALS MARGREID
NUSSERHOF
PACHERHOF
PETER DIPOLI
PFITSCHER
REVÌ TRENTODOC
SCHINTERHOF
STROBLHOF
TASCHLERHOF
TENUTA J. HOFSTATTER
TENUTA SAN LEONARDO
TIEFENBRUNNER
WALDGRIES

THE ADRIATIC COAST

EMILIA-ROMAGNA
CANTINA DELLA VOLTA
CANTINA PALTRINIERI
CLETO CHIARLI
COSTA ARCHI
ENIO OTTAVIANI
LA STOPPA
LA TOSA
NOELIA RICCI
PODERE IL SALICETO

MARCHE
AURORA
BISCI
CA'LIPTRA
CANTINA CAVALIERI DI BENEDET
    GABRIELE
CANTINA SANTA BARBARA
COL DI CORTE
COLLE STEFANO
DIANETTI VINI
FATTORIA CORONCINO
FATTORIA NANNÌ
FATTORIA SAN LORENZO
FELICI
LA MARCA DI SAN MICHELE
LA MONACESCA VINI
LA STAFFA
MARIA PIA CASTELLI
OASI DEGLI ANGELI DI ROSSI ELEONORA
PANTALEONE
PIEVALTA
PODERI MATTIOLI
PODERI SAN LAZZARO
VALTER MATTONI
VILLA BUCCI

ABRUZZO
AMOROTTI
AZIENDA AGRICOLA PETTINELLA
    VINEYARD
CATALDI MADONNA
CIAVOLICH
COLLE FLORIDO
EMIDIO PEPE
FATTORIA NICODEMI
FEUDO ANTICO
IMPRESSIONI GIANNI SINESI
NICOLETTA DE FERMO
ORLANDI CONTUCCI PONNO
PRAESIDIUM
TIBERIO
TORRE DEI BEATI
VALENTINI
VALLE REALE
VINI PETINELLA

THE AMALFI COAST

CAMPANIA
AGNANUM
BENITO FERRARA
CANTINA MARISA CUOMO
CANTINE ASTRONI
CANTINE I FAVATI
CIRO PICARIELLO
DELL'ANGELO
DI PRISCO
DONNA ELVIRA
GALARDI
GUIDO MARSELLA
I BORBONI
LE ORMERE
LUIGI MAFFINI
MASSERIA FELICIA
MONTEVETRANO
NANNI COPÈ
PERILLO
PIERLUIGI ZAMPAGLIONE
PIETRACUPA
PODERE MELONE
QUINTODECIMO
SAN SALVATORE
SCALA FENICIA
TENUTA MADRE
TENUTA SAN FRANCESCO
TENUTA SCUOTTO

FRIULI

BORGO DEL TIGLIO
DAMIJAN PODVERSIC
DORO PRINCIC
EDI KANTE
EDI KEBER
GRAVNER VINI
I CLIVI
IL CARPINO
LA CASTELLADA
LE DUE TERRE
MARCO SARA
MARIO SCHIOPETTO
MARTISSIMA
MIANI
MITJA SIRK
PRIMOSIC
RONCO DEL GNEMIZ
RONCO SEVERO
RONCÚS
SKERK
TOROS
VENICA & VENICA
VIGNA PETRUSSA
VIGNAI DA DULINE
ZIDARICH

THE ITALIAN LAKES

LAKE MAGGIORE
ANTICHI VIGNETI DI CANTALUPO
ANTONIOLO
LA PREVOSTURA
MURAJE
NERVI CONTERNO
PROPRIETÀ SPERINO
TRAVAGLINI GIANCARLO GATTINARA

LAKE ISEO AND LAKE COMO
CANTINA PAGNONCELLI FOLCIERI

LAKE GARDA
ALESSANDRA DIVELLA
ANDRE ARICI–AZIENDA AGRICOLA

COLLINE DELLA STELLA
ARCARI E DANESI
AZIENDA AGRICOLA CAVALLERI
BELLAVISTA
BERLUCCHI

CA' DEL BOSCO
CAMOSSI
CASCINA MADDALENA
CORTE FUSIA
FACCOLI FRANCIACORTA
FILIPPO BIANCHI
I BARISÈI
IL PENDIO
MOSNEL
OTTELLA

OLTREPÒ PAVESE
BALLABIO
CA' DEL CONTE
LINO MAGA
MARCHESI DI MONTALTO
TENUTA MAZZOLINO

LAZIO AND UMBRIA

LAZIO
ANTICHE CANTINE MIGLIACCIO
ANTONELLI MARCO
AZIENDA BIOLOGICA DE SANCTIS
DAMIANO CIOLLI
FAMIGLIA COTARELLA
SAN GIOVENALE
TENUTA DI FIORANO
TENUTA LA PAZZAGLIA

UMBRIA
ANTICA AZIENDA AGRICOLA
    PAOLO BEA
BARBERANI
BOCALE VALENTINI
CANTINA FONGOLI
CANTINA PALAZZONE ORVIETO
CANTINA PERTICAIA
CANTINA ROCCAFIORE
CASTELLO DELLA SALA
DECUGNANO DEI BARBI
FATTORIA MANI DI LUNA
LEONARDO BUSSOLETTI
RAÍNA
TENUTA ALFREDOSA
TENUTA BELLAFONTE

LIGURIA AND SARDINIA

LIGURIA
BIO VIO
ELIO ALTARE
FORLINI CAPPELLINI
LAURA ASCHERO
MACCARIO DRINGENBERG
OTTAVIANO LAMBRUSCHI
TERENZUOLA

SARDINIA
AGRICOLA PUNICA
CANTINA DEPPERU
CANTINA GIBA
CANTINA GIOVANNI MONTISCI
CANTINA MURALES
CAPICHERA
GABBAS
GIUSEPPE SEDILESU
LUCA GUNGUI
MALVASIA DI BOSA–CANTINA
    GIOVANNI BATTISTA COLUMBU
MORA E MEMO
PRANU TUVARA
PUSOLE
QUARTOMORO
SIDDÙRA
TANI
TENUTA MASONE MANNU
VIGNE SURRAU

PIEDMONT

BAROLO
AGRICOLA BRANDINI
AZELIA DI LUIGI SCAVINO
AZIENDA AGRICOLA GILLARDI
AZIENDA AGRICOLA PECCHENINO
BARTOLO MASCARELLO
BORGOGNO
BRICCOLINA
BROVIA
BURLOTTO
CAPPELLANO
CASCINA BALLARIN
CASCINA FONTANA
CHIARA BOSCHIS
CONTERNO FANTINO
CORINO GIOVANNI

DIEGO CONTERNO
DOMENICO CLERICO
ELIO ALTARE
ELIO GRASSO
ELIO SANDRI
ELVIO COGNO
ETTORE GERMANO
FIGLI LUIGI ODDERO
FRATELLI ALESSANDRIA
G. D. VAJRA
GIACOMO CONTERNO
GIACOMO FENOCCHIO
GIACOMO GRIMALDI
GIOVANNI CANONICA
GIOVANNI ROSSO
GIULIA NEGRI
GIUSEPPE RINALDI
LIVIA FONTANA
LORENZO ACCOMASSO
LUCIANO SANDRONE
LUIGI BAUDANA
MARCARINI
MARZIANO ABBONA
MASCARELLO
MASSOLINO
MAURO MOLINO
MAURO VEGLIO
MICHELE CHIARLO
ODDERO
PAOLO SCAVINO
PODERI ALDO CONTERNO
PRINCIPIANO FERDINANDO
ROBERTO VOERZIO
SCARPA
TREDIBERRI
UGO LEQUIO
VIETTI

BARBARESCO
ALBINO ROCCA
BRUNO GIACOSA
BRUNO ROCCA
CA' DEL BAIO
CANTINA DEL PINO
CANTINA RIZZI
CANTINE DEL GLICINE
CARLO GIACOSA
CASCINA DELLE ROSE
CASCINA MORASSINO
CERETTO
AZIENDE VITIVINICOLE CIGLIUTI
GAJA
GIUSEPPE CORTESE
LA CA' NÖVA
LA SPINETTA
MOCCAGATTA

NADA FIORENZO
PELISSERO
PIERO BUSSO
PRODUTTORI DEL BARBARESCO
RIVELLA SERAFINO
RIVELLA SILVIA
ROAGNA
TENUTE CISA ASINARI DEI
    MARCHESI DI GRÉSY

OTHER PIEDMONTESE DOCS AND DOCGS
ACCORNERO VINI
ALTARE NICHOLAS
BENITO FAVARO
CAS'AL'MAT
CASCINA GENTILE
CLAUDIO MARIOTTO
CONTRATTO
COPPO
EMILIO VADA
GHIOMO
GIOVANNI ALMONDO
I PARCELLARI
LE PIANE
MALVIRÀ
MATTEO CORREGGIA
NICOLA BERGAGLIO
POMODOLCE
REPETTO VINI
SAN FEREOLO
VIGNE MARINA COPPI
VIGNETI MASSA
VILLA SPARINA

SICILY

ETNA
BENANTI
CALABRETTA VINI
CANTINA MAUGERI
EDUARDO TORRES ACOSTA
EMILIANO FALSINI
FEDERICO GRAZIANI
FRANK CORNELISSEN
GIROLAMO RUSSO
GRACII VIGNERI DI SALVO FOTI
IDDA
PASSOPISCIARO
PIETRADOLCE
SANTA MARIA LA NAVE
TENUTA DELLE TERRE NERE
TENUTA DI FESSINA
TENUTE BOSCO

TORNATORE WINE

MARSALA
CANTINE FLORIO
FRANCESCO INTORCIA
MARCO DE BARTOLI
VITO CURATOLO

PANTELLERIAS
FERRANDES
SALVATORE MURANA VINI
SOLIDEA VINI
TENUTA REKHALE

THE AEOLIAN ISLANDS:
SALINA AND LIPARI
CANTINE COLOSI
CARAVAGLIO
HAUNER

OTHER SICILIAN IGTS, DOCS, AND DOCGS
AZIENDA AGRICOLA ARIANNA OCCHIPINTI
BARONE DI SERRAMARROCCO
BARONI DI PIANOGRILLO
BONAVITA
CASE ALTE
CASTELLUCCI MIANO
CENTOPASSI
COS
FEUDI DEL PISCIOTTO
FEUDO DISISA
FONDO DEI BARBERA
FRANCESCO GUCCIONE
GULFI CANTINA
LE CASEMATTE
MARABINO
MORGANTE
PALARI
TENUTA SAN GIAIME

THE SOUTH

MOLISE
CLAUDIO CIPRESSI

BASILICATA
AZIENDA AGRICOLA ELENA FUCCI
BASILISCO VINI
CAMERLENGO VINO
CANTINE DEL NOTAIO
GRIFALCO VINI
MASSERIA CROCCO
MUSTO CARMELITANO

CANTINE DEL NOTAIO
GRIFALCO VINI
MASSERIA CROCCO
MUSTO CARMELITANO
PATERNOSTER
RIPANERO

PUGLIA
CANTINE MENHIR SALENTO
CANTINE PALLOTTA
FATALONE
GIANFRANCO FINO VITICOLTORE
HISOTELARAY
MORELLA
SAN MARZANO VINI
SEVERINO GAROFANO
VIGNETI REALE

CALABRIA
'A VITA
CANTINE VIOLA
CATALDO CALABRETTA
CERAUDO
GIUSEPPE CALABRESE
MASSERIA PERUGINI
SERGIO ARCURI
SPIRITI EBBRI

TUSCANY

BRUNELLO DI MONTALCINO
ARGIANO
BIONDI SANTI
CASANOVA DI NERI
CASTELLO TRICERCHI
CERBAIONA
FATTOI
FATTORIA DEL PINO
FULIGNI
GIANFRANCO SOLDERA
IL COLLE
IL MARRONETO
LA CERBAIOLA
L'AIETTA
LE CHIUSE
LE MACIOCHE
LE POTAZZINE
LE RAGNAIE
PIETROSO
PIEVE SANTA RESTITUTA
POGGIO DI SOTTO
RIDOLFI MONTALCINO

SALVIONI
SAN GUGLIELMO
SAN LORENZO
SIRO PACENTI
TALENTI MONTALCINO
TASSI MONTALCINO
TENUTA IL POGGIONE

CHIANTI
CANTINA RIPOLI
CASTELL'IN VILLA
CASTELLO DEI RAMPOLLA
CASTELLO DI AMA
CASTELLO DI MONSANTO
CASTELLO DI VOLPAIA
FATTORIA DI LAMOLE
FATTORIA POGGERINO
FATTORIA SAN GIUSTO
    A RENTENNANO
FATTORIA SELVAPIANA
FONTODI
FRESCOBALDI
ISOLE E OLENA
ISTINE
LE CINCIOLE
MARCHESI ANTINORI
MAURIZIO ALONGI
MONTERAPONI
MONTEVERTINE
PODERE POGGIO SCALETTE
QUERCIABELLA
TENUTA DI CARLEONE
VIGNAVECCHIA

BOLGHERI
CA'MARCANDA
CHIAPPINI
FABIO MOTTA
GRATTAMACCO
GUADO AL TASSO
I LUOGHI
LE MACCHIOLE
MASSETO
MICHELE SATTA
ORNELLAIA
TENUTA SAN GUIDO

OTHER TUSCAN IGTS,
DOCS, AND DOCGS
AMPELEIA
ANTONIO CAMILLO
ASCIONE-ALONGI
AZIENDA AGRICOLA TOSCANI
AZIENDA VITIVINICOLA DUEMANI
BOSCARELLI
COLLE MASSARI

FATTORIA LE PUPILLE
IL COLOMBAIO DI SANTA CHIARA
MONTENIDOLI
PETROLO
PODERE 414
PODERE CASANOVA
PODERE DELLA CIVETTAJA
POLIZIANO
ROCCAPESTA
TENIMENTI D'ALESSANDRO
TENUTA DI TRINORO
TENUTA DI VALGIANO
TERENZI
TUA RITA

THE VENETO

ALLEGRINI
ANSELMI
ANTOLINI VINI
AZIENDA AGRICOLA
    BUSSOLA TOMMASO
BELE CASEL
BERTANI
BISOL 1542
CA' RUGATE
CA' LA BIONDA
DAL FORNO ROMANO
FILIPPI
FONGARO
GINI VINI
GIUSEPPE QUINTARELLI
GRAZIANO PRÀ
INAMA
LA GIUVA
LE RAGOSE
LE SALETTE
MONTE DALL'ORA
MONTE DEI RAGNI
NEVIO SCALA
NINO FRANCO
PASQUA VIGNETI E CANTINA
PIEROPAN
ROCCOLO GRASSI
SUAVIA
VIGNETI DI ETTORE
VILLA CALICANTUS

Endless vineyard views in the Piedmont region.

ACKNOWLEDGMENTS

My thanks to all the winegrowers and winemakers who have welcomed me
with such warmth, modesty, and generosity. Thank you for your time,
your stories, your wines, and your vineyards, which you constantly enrich
through your work and care.

Thanks to Mary Bernardo, my sister and my great companion, with whom I
so often share my journeys through the world of wine, for infusing our travels
with her lightheartedness, effervescence, and taste for life.

Thanks to Bruno Tessarech, the friend who, with his graciousness, empathy,
and sensitivity, ensures the quality of my prose, bringing the depth and breadth
of his philosophy to the grand journey that is writing.
Thanks to all the friends with whom I have so often had the good fortune
to enjoy a fine glass of champagne.

Thanks to Prosper, Martine, and the entire team at Assouline,
whose wholehearted professionalism has enabled me to share
my thoughts with our readers.

And finally, thanks to my parents, all my sisters, and my brother,
whom I can always count on, driven as I am by my uncertainty,
to keep me moving forward.

Strolling around the vineyards of Cantina Mir, a winery in the heart of Puglia.

ABOUT THE AUTHOR

Enrico Bernardo made his name at Le V, the restaurant at the Four Seasons George V in Paris, and was named Best Sommelier of the World in 2004. As a restaurateur, he has created and owned several Michelin-star-holding restaurants, focused on pairing the perfect wine with each dish. Bernardo consults for food, wine, and art de vivre companies worldwide and is the author of several books, including *The Impossible Collection of Wine* (2016), *La Sagesse du Vin* (2021), and *The Impossible Collection of Champagne* (2022). In 2018, he undertook a world wine trip, broadening his knowledge of the industry and bringing unknown talents to light.

CREDITS:

Assouline supports *One Tree Planted* in its commitment to create a more sustainable world through reforestation.

Front cover design: © Assouline Publishing.
Back cover tip-on (clockwise from top left): © Gilbert Bages; © Enrico Costantini; © Decugnano dei Barbi; © Slim Aarons/Getty Images
Endpages: Design © Assouline
Regional Maps: © Thibault Bouisset
Map of Italy (p.4): © Valeria Ramírez Reyes

© 2024 Assouline Publishing
3 Park Avenue, 27th floor
New York, NY 10016 USA
Tel: 212-989-6769 Fax: 212-647-0005
assouline.com

Editor: Léana Esch
Art directors: Sebastien Ratto-Viviani, Winnie Lu
Designer: Florence Reynier
Photo editor: Muse Giacalone

Printed in Italy by Grafiche Milani
ISBN: 9781649804181
10 9 8 7 6 5 4 3 2

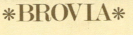

TIGNANELLO

Vino prodotto con uve Sangiovese e, in piccola parte, Cabernet nell'antico podere sito nel cuore della Toscana, di proprietà dei Marchesi Antinori di Firenze, viticoltori dal 1385. Il terreno, in collina, è composto da roccia di "Galestro" e "Alberese"

ha un' esposizione a solatio ed un' altitudine che va dai 350 ai 400 metri sul livello del mare. Il vino è invecchiato esclusivamente in piccole botti di rovere pregiate e successivamente affinato in bottiglia.

TOSCANA
INDICAZIONE GEOGRAFICA TIPICA

Marchesi
ANTINORI

BROVIA

NULLAM SACRA VITE PRIUS SEVERIS ARBOREM

BAROLO
DENOMINAZIONE DI ORIGINE CONTROLLATA E GARANTITA
BREA

SOLAIA
Marchesi Antinori
Firenze

2021
Fausto
VIGNE MARINA COPPI
Colli Tortonesi
Denominazione di Origine Controllata
Timorasso

CONT...
BAR...
DENOMINAZIONE DI ORIG...
RISE...
Mo...
IMBOTTIGLI...
AZIENDA AG...
GIACOMO CONTERNO d...
MONFORTE...
0,75 l℮   PRODO

ANTINORI

MasoMartis
BLANC DE BLANCS
BRUT
TRENTODOC

IL RADDESE
1876

GRAN SELEZIONE
CHIANTI CLASSICO
Vendemmia 2021
Radda

Imbottigliato all'origine dalla
AZIENDA AGRICOLA
VALENTINI
s.s. società agricola
Loreto Aprutino - PE - Italia
12,5% vol
℮ 75 cl

Vendemmia 1995

PRODOTTO IN ITALIA

Trebbiano
d'Abruzzo
denominazione di origine controllata

L. 4.07   CONTIENE SOLFITI

SASSICAIA
1985
TENUTA SAN GUIDO

Imbottigliato all'origine dal produttore
Tenuta San Guido - Bolgheri (107 LI)

VIGNETO
19...
B...
Denominazione di Origin...
Imbottigliato all'origine...
Cascina Nuova...
Elio Altar...
Fraz. Annunziata

Poggio di Sotto
Riserva 1997
Castelnuovo dell'Abate
Montalcino Italia

BRUNELLO DI MONTALCINO
Denominazione di Origine Controllata e Garantita
Imbottigliato all'origine da P. Palmucci per
Collemassari Spa Società Agricola nella Tenuta
Poggio di Sotto

VALTELLINA SUPERIORE
DENOMINAZIONE DI ORIGINE CONTROLLATA E GARANTITA

RISERVA
2016

Grumello
Buon Consiglio
ARPEPE

GUIDORICCIO DA FOGLIANO
1990
CASTELLO DI AMA®
CHIANTI CLASSICO
DENOMINAZIONE DI ORIGINE CONTROLLATA E GARANTITA
bottiglia n°
097574
ESTATE BOTTLED BY CASTELLO DI AMA S.p.A.
IN CHIANTI - ITALY
...CT OF ITALY - ALC. 12.5% BY VOL

Vigna del Sorbo
Chianti Classico
DENOMINAZIONE DI ORIGINE
CONTROLLATA E GARANTITA
Gran Selezione
PANZANO
2020
FONTODI

BARBARES...
Denominazione di Origine Controllata e...
AS...
F...
CA' DEL
AZIENDA AG...
Imbottigliato all'origine da | Estate bottled by:
di Giulio Grasso - Treiso (cn) Italia - Pro...
Contiene solfiti / Contains sulphites / C...
Enthält Sulfite / Inde...

CONTERNO

Amarone della Valpolicella
denominazione di origine controllata
classico superiore
1978
Imbottigliato all'origine
nell'azienda agricola
Quintarelli Giuseppe
Cerè di Negrar - Italia
ottenuto da uve scelte coltivate sul
monte la Paletta ed appassite
secondo tradizione
0,750 LT.℮   15% Vol.

Ronco del Gnemiz
Friuli Colli Orientali
Chardonnay 2019
RONCO BASSO

BAROLO
DENOMINAZIONE DI ORIGINE CONTROLLATA E GARANTITA
FRANCIA
2018
IMBOTTIGLIATO ALL'ORIGINE DA
AZIENDA VITIVINICOLA
GIACOMO CONTERNO di GIOVANNI CONTERNO s.a.s.s.
MONFORTE D'ALBA - ITALIA

DIEGO CONTE...